Cultural Perception of Marriage among Muslims

the institutions of marriage

www.gatewaytoilm.com

بِسْمِ ٱللَّهِ ٱلرَّحْمَٰنِ ٱلرَّحِيمِ

SHEIKH MOHAMMAD KAMALUDIN

Table of Contents

Acknowledgements i
Preface iii
Introduction vii
Authors Perception xi
In the Beginning 1
Marriage as an Institution 5
Walliship 6
Who is the Walli? 7
Finding a Partner 9
Consent 11
Choosing a Husband 14
The Husband's Duties 17
Sexual Etiquettes 20
The Wife's Duties 27
Conclusion 31
Relationship outside Marriage 35
Talaaq / Divorce 37
Some reasons for Divorce 39
Arbitration 45

The Effects of Divorce on the Family	48
Case Study 1	51
Case Study 2	59
Case Study 3	69
Case Study 4	83
Warning against Anger	101
The Purification of the Heart from Anger without Grounds	101
The Cure for Anger	111
The Tongue	115
Conclusion	117
Glossary	119

Sheikh Mohammad Kamaludin

Acknowledgements

I would like to express my sincere gratitude and thanks to Br. Sayed Abdul Rahman and Br. Ayoube aka Tag for their technical contributions and immense help and encouragement, in developing this book and to Br Ismail Bowman and my son Ibrahim for proof reading, and Br Alfa for his technical and formatting contribution of this book.

Preface

<u>I would respectfully ask that because this book contains verses of scriptures it should not be place in an unclean environment.</u>

As a result of the responses I received from some of the readers of my last book "Love and Mercy" regarding the benefits they have received. This has driven me to produce "Cultural Perception of Marriage among Muslims" as a followup, which offers an in-depth and comprehensive understanding of Married regulation drawn from the scriptures and the scholars of this institution, plus the knowledge gained for many years of experience as a married consular, while highlighting married relationship from an Islamic perspective.

I have also brought evidence of the difference between the guidance, the rules and regulations offered by the Creator of this institution, and exemplified by the Prophet of Islam and his Companions which guarantee a blissful married life, and the destructive innovated cultural practices drawn from national, tribal, and traditional customs, and its evil consequences.

For the Purpose of beneficial knowledge and education are some explanations and examples of how to avoid and overcome some of the difficulties of married life, accompanied with a vivid explanation of the Fiqh of marriage drawn from the book and the Sunnah (pbuh) while highlighting some of the pitfalls and the snares that lie in the path of marital relationship, engineered by Iblis the devout enemy of humans.

I have also included three separate interviews and case studies of married couples who have gone through the fitnah of divorce and its disadvantages, and some classical examples of solutions to marital problems rather than resorting to divorce which is lawful but is hated by Allah.

It is my hope that these examples that are drawn from the guidance of our beloved Prophet Mohammed (pbuh) and His wives which has been left for all people will be of great benefit to the true seeker of knowledge.

For the benefit of my readers I have chosen to include the manager of Anger in this book for although anger is one of the attributes given to human by our

Creator, its application can result either praiseworthily or blameworthy, and when it is used in a negative and explosive manner, the consequence can have a destructive effect upon it's recipient, to the extent that it results in either be death or destruction.

It is therefore of paramount importance that one should seek the knowledge for the treatment, control, and cure of anger, and how it can be use in a positive, healthy and praiseworthy way that is beneficial and pleasing to Allah.

Muhammad Kamaludin.

الحمد لله نحمده ونستعينه ونستغفره ونعوذ بالله من شرور أنفسنا، ومن سيئات أعمالنا، من يهده الله فلا مضل له، ومن يضلل فلا هادي له، وأشهد أن لا إله إلا الله وحده لا شريك له، وأشهد أن محمداً عبده ورسوله

We praise Allah, seek His help and ask His forgiveness. We seek refuge with Allah from the evils of ourselves and from our bad actions. Whoever Allah guides no one can lead astray. Whoever Allah leads astray, no one can guide. I testify there is no deity worthy of worship except Allah alone without any partners, and I testify that Muhammad (pbuh) is His slave servant and messenger.

﴿ يَٰٓأَيُّهَا ٱلَّذِينَ ءَامَنُوا۟ ٱتَّقُوا۟ ٱللَّهَ حَقَّ تُقَاتِهِۦ وَلَا تَمُوتُنَّ إِلَّا وَأَنتُم مُّسْلِمُونَ

Oh ye who believe! Fear Allah as He should be feared and die not except in a state of. (3/102).

O mankind! Be careful of your duty to your Lord who created you from a single soul and from it created its mate and from them twain hath spread abroad a multitude of men and women. Be careful of your duty toward the wombs (that bare you). Lo! Allah hath been a watcher over you.

يَٰٓأَيُّهَا ٱلَّذِينَ ءَامَنُوا۟ ٱتَّقُوا۟ ٱللَّهَ وَقُولُوا۟ قَوْلًا سَدِيدًا ﴿ ٧٠ ﴾ يُصْلِحْ لَكُمْ أَعْمَٰلَكُمْ وَيَغْفِرْ لَكُمْ ذُنُوبَكُمْ ۗ وَمَن يُطِعِ ٱللَّهَ وَرَسُولَهُۥ فَقَدْ فَازَ فَوْزًا عَظِيمًا

Sheikh Mohammad Kamaludin

O ye who believe! Fear Allah, and (always) say a word directed to the truth. He may make your conduct whole and sound and forgive you your sins. He who obeys Allah and the Apostle has already attained the highest achievement. (33/70 & 71

Introduction

One of the reasons that drove me to write Love and Mercy was based upon experience and knowledge gained over the past thirty years while working in Muslim communities both at home and abroad.

As a new Muslim I became fearful and frightened regarding the extent to which Biddah became accepted, tolerated, practiced, and taken for granted that whenever I tried to reintroduce certain Sunnah I would be criticised for interfering in the culture of these people. It is shameful and regrettable that a larger percentage of the Muslims from all over the world who have had the religion of Islam for hundreds of years have mixed up and assimilated their cultural, and traditional customs into the Islamic code of practice.

These Biddah covers many aspects of worship, but the one that I will focus on is that which relates to marriage in Islam, for too often instead of resorting to the Book and the Sunnah and consensus of the scholars when dealing with marital issues, solutions are often drawn from their innovated, cultural, tribal, and traditional practices.

It is also my experience that with respect to many acts of worship the Sunnah of the Messenger of Allah (pbuh) has become so polluted with innovation that I have come to understand why the scholars of Islam who have stated that If the of the Messenger of Allah (pbuh) should return to us today with exception of parts of the salat they do not think they would recognise the Islam that is being practiced by the Muslims of today to be the same as the Islam that was taught by the Prophet(pbuh) and practiced by his companions"

These instilled rulings and traditions which are neither drawn from the Book of Allah or the Sunnah of His Messenger Muhammad (pbuh), nor the consensus of the scholars going back to the companions of the Prophet (pbuh), are passed on from the elders of the communities to the younger generation which in many cases are serious innovations, eventually leads to varying degrees of conconflict between them and the people who are upon the Sunnah of Resole Allah (pbuh) when trying to find Islamic solutions to address marital issues or problems.

Cultural Perception of Marriage among Muslims

As for the new Muslims who are not capable to deduce from the text of the Sunnah and the rulings of the Scholars the correct understanding and rulings of the Shariah, I saw it as a necessity to do this research taken from the Book and the Sunnah and the Scholars of Al us Sunnah wal Jamaah to help us to have a better and clearer understanding of some of the correct rulings that Allah and His Rasoul has prescribed for all Muslims irrespective of nationalities or ethnicity when dealing with marital issues.

It is therefore plain to be seen that the reasons why the Islamic criteria have not remained as the basis upon which solutions are sought to address marital problems is because many Muslim families, communities, and nations have either deviated from, have never studied, or do not go back to the Sharia, or consult the people of knowledge to ascertain the correct rulings that Allah has given us Muslims as the only correct way to address or deal with our worldly problems be it religious or secular, in other words matters of the Deen or matters of the Dunya.

With this understanding I concluded that the only sensible solution to this problem is first to address its cause, and if this is done it should take care of it's effects. Let me also add that, whoever fear Allah and the last day, should listen carefully to the advice given to us from the Lord of the world.

يَٰٓأَيُّهَا ٱلَّذِينَ ءَامَنُوٓاْ أَطِيعُواْ ٱللَّهَ وَأَطِيعُواْ ٱلرَّسُولَ وَأُوْلِي ٱلْأَمْرِ مِنكُمْ فَإِن تَنَٰزَعْتُمْ فِى شَىْءٍ فَرُدُّوهُ إِلَى ٱللَّهِ وَٱلرَّسُولِ إِن كُنتُمْ تُؤْمِنُونَ بِٱللَّهِ وَٱلْيَوْمِ ٱلْءَاخِرِ ذَٰلِكَ خَيْرٌ وَأَحْسَنُ تَأْوِيلًا (٥٩)

"O you, who have believed, obey Allah and obey the Messenger and those in authority among you. And if you disagree over anything, refer it to Allah and the Messenger, if you should believe in Allah and the Last Day. That is the best and best in result" (4:59)

And now that the Holy Prophet has died, we refer it to the Quran and his Sunnah (PBUH) and the consensus of the Ullamah. It is Allah who initiated the institution of marriage and has made 'rights and obligations' one of the most fundamental criteria upon which its relationship is based, we will always have to resort to the Book of Allah and the Sunnah of His Prophet (PBUH) and the understanding of the Salaf and nothing else when we are looking for

Sheikh Mohammad Kamaludin

solutions to address marital issues.

As an incentive to us reverts to Islam, one of our respected Shaikh from Saudi Arabia, Abdul Salam Burgees (Ra) mentioned during one of his lectures in the Brixton Masjid that he was amazed at the level of understanding and practices of the new Muslims he met in London which in many cases are superior to the Muslims in his own country who had lived and practice Islam for centuries.

He further said it took him some time to figure out and understand the reasons behind such a rapid development in such a short space of time. Finally, he concluded that us the new Muslims came into Islam without any instilled tribal, cultural, or traditional hang-ups or obligations which have caused many nations and tribes to become confused and misguided in distinguishing the Islamic rulings from their traditional and cultural way of life of life of a Muslim.

Rather, he said he has concluded that we entered Islam fully, read the correct books such as the Quran, Hadith, books of Tawheed and Fiqh etc., while we sought out, found and kept in touch with the scholars of Islam and their students, and this being the case we rightly guided.

May Allah bless the Shaykh and reward him with Jannah for his contribution to the purity of our religion based upon the Book and the Sunnah of our beloved Prophet and the Manhaj of the Salaf. Ameen.

In my research what I discovered was that these elders and chiefs in their respective community instead of going back to the Book and the Sunnah when making judgements on a matter that should be dealt with according to the rulings of the Sharia, they would resort to their own Tribal, Cultural and Traditional rulings.

Muslims who subscribe to such authority are often unjust and can only be described as a people who are in a state of loss. When these misguidances are passed on to the younger generation via the elders, many are the times when all the tribes or in some cases the whole Muslim nation end up with a culture that is based upon innovation thinking that these rulings are drawn from the Islamic Sharia.

For the benefit of my readers, I would like to add two quotes from two of our most eminent scholars of Islam.

It is reported that Baath in (al-Ibantul Kubraa. No. 162) said that it reached him that Omar Ibn al-Khattab rh. The Emier al-Mumineen for anyone going astray thinking that he is not upon guidance, nor for abandoning guidance thinking he is upon misguidance. Since the affairs have been made clear, the proof established, and the excuse cut off.

That is because the Sunnah and the Jemaah have consolidated and safeguarded all the religion. It is having been made clear to the people. So, it is upon the people to comply and follow.

In another interesting reminder from our sheikh Imam Az-Zuhree, (May Allah be pleased with him) one of the great Imams of the past.

He said: "It is the role of Allah (s a) to send down the revelation".

It is the duty of the Prophets to communicate and convey the message.

It is for us to accept it. (Submit)

Authors Perception

First, I believe peace and security is a necessity that is sought after by human society, and for which international conferences and seminars gatherings are held to accumulate all the mental and physical energies in its pursuit.

Secondly, the attainment of peace, trust, and security, in any society is considered being necessity and sometimes takes precedence even over the necessity of food. For this reason, Islam has taken care to bring about its cause and means by first and foremost building man's faith, behaviour, and character. Man is a member of the society in which he lives, and he lies at the core of the interaction of that society.

Therefore, he is most in need of himself being educated and brought up properly (Allah fearing) so that he becomes a just person whose faith will keep him from aggression and crimes against others in this society.

At the same time, it is not possible that one should live according to Islamic laws and manage his affairs according to Islamic principle if the basic building block of the society is not based upon a firm and correct foundation (i.e.) correct Aqedah, and adhering to the Sunnah of the Prophet (pbuh) with the correct understanding of the Salaf which prepares such an individual for that life, and gets him or ready for a pious environment. This will help him or her to mould this noble character, which can only be achieved by emulating the examples of our Holy Prophet Mohammed (pbuh), based upon the statement of Allah concerning him.

Certainly, you have in the Messenger of Allah an excellent example for him who hopes in Allah and the latter day and remembers Allah much. HQ 32/

Also, in another address Allah (pbuh) has told us.

وَإِنَّكَ لَعَلَىٰ خُلُقٍ عَظِيمٍ) ٤

Surely, thou (Muhammad (pbuh) hast sublime morals (68/4)

The family is the cornerstone and basic building block of which societies are made. The stronger the family is and the more it adheres to the ethical principles of the Sharia based upon the rights and obligations prescribed by Allah for his (ABD) servants, the more that will be reflected on society. That being the case honour, dignity and ethical behaviour, as well as peace, tranquillity and steadfastness will be guaranteed.

However, on the other hand the more the stronghold of the family becomes fragmented and broken up, and vice and immorality can infiltrate it, then the situation of the society as a whole will reflect the behaviour of its families.

In the Beginning

Based upon man's first experience of being deceived by the Devil, Allah advised mankind in general.

يَٰبَنِىٓ ءَادَمَ لَا يَفْتِنَنَّكُمُ ٱلشَّيْطَٰنُ كَمَآ أَخْرَجَ أَبَوَيْكُم مِّنَ ٱلْجَنَّةِ يَنزِعُ عَنْهُمَا لِبَاسَهُمَا لِيُرِيَهُمَا سَوْءَٰتِهِمَآ ۗ إِنَّهُۥ يَرَىٰكُمْ هُوَ وَقَبِيلُهُۥ مِنْ حَيْثُ لَا تَرَوْنَهُمْ ۗ إِنَّا جَعَلْنَا ٱلشَّيَٰطِينَ أَوْلِيَآءَ لِلَّذِينَ لَا يُؤْمِنُونَ (٢٧)

Oh, Children of Adam! Let not Satan seduce you as he caused your (first) parents to go forth from the Garden and to reoff from them their robe (of innocence) that he might manifest their shame to them. Lo! He See'eth you he and his tribe, from whence ye see him not. Lo! We have made the devils protecting friends for those who believe not. (7/27)

The woman was created by Allah, and she been given four possessions reflecting her role in the family. (1) Mother, (2) Daughter, (3) Sister, and (4) Wife. Likewise, 1 the man, who has the same Creator, has been given his role in the family and can only function as, (1) Father, (2) Son, (3) Brother, and (4) Husband. That being the case, the two important issues that I will try to address in this narrative are our responsibilities towards our wives and our mothers.

Permit me to say that I find the Holy Quran to be the mother of all the sciences of life, and from it springs forth the different sciences of living as have been exemplified in the Sunnah of our beloved Prophet Mohammed (pbuh).

Therefore, I will address each subject as one of the sciences of human relati0n. Hence marriage being one of the sciences in Islam should be studied by the people who are about to become involved in this relationship, in order to find out and to understand the protocols of marriage life that has being ordained by the Creator of this institution.

Also, all the people who are already involved in a marital relationship and have not familiarise themselves with the correct understanding of this great science, should take some time out to acquaint themselves with what is of them to be that wife or husband that is able to fulfil the rights and obligations of each other.

Also, since Allah has made the lawful reproduction of humans to be generated through marital relationship, the couple should learn and teach their children their obligations to their parents, respective members of the family, elders, respect for the rule of law, and their teachers etc. which Allah has made obligatory on all mankind.

Only when this is observed and put into practice, this relation will be enhanced blissfully, and we would have made our contributions to a society in which the fear of Allah become the foundation upon which the human relation relationship is based. A proof of this understanding is based upon the statement of Allah:

يَٰٓأَيُّهَا ٱلنَّاسُ ٱتَّقُوا۟ رَبَّكُمُ ٱلَّذِى خَلَقَكُم مِّن نَّفْسٍ وَٰحِدَةٍ وَخَلَقَ مِنْهَا زَوْجَهَا وَبَثَّ مِنْهُمَا رِجَالًا كَثِيرًا وَنِسَآءً ۚ وَٱتَّقُوا۟ ٱللَّهَ ٱلَّذِى تَسَآءَلُونَ بِهِۦ وَٱلْأَرْحَامَ ۚ إِنَّ ٱللَّهَ كَانَ عَلَيْكُمْ رَقِيبًا

O mankind! Be dutiful to your Lord, who created you from a single person (Adam), and from him (Adam) He created his wife [Hawwa (Eve)], and from them both He created many men and women and fear Allah through Whom you demand your mutual (rights), and do not cut the relations of the wombs (kinship). Surely, Allah is Ever an All-Watcher over you. (4/1)

There is a principle in the fundamentals of the religion of Islam that to be successful in any matter, knowledge must precede the action. It is therefore expedient that who is about to become involved in a marital relationship should pay strict attention to the above-mentioned verse of the Holy Quran, since it contains one of the most valuable advice regarding the rights and the obligations of wife, the husband and the extended family throughout their married life.

We should also be conscious of the fact that we cannot hide in the darkest crevice of the earth and abuse each other feeling safe that we have not been seen, for the One through whom we claim our mutual rights is a constant watcher over us.

It is also extremely important that this advice in the Holy Quran is not only addressing Muslims as some may be led to believe because the information is coming from the Quran.

However, when Allah wish to address the Muslims, He would say oh believers, but in this case, he says "Oh mankind" which is an address to all human bean since He Allah is the Creator of humans, and it is He who initiated the institution of marriage, through which the Lawful reproduction of humans takes place.

So, the Holy Quran being the final revelation to mankind and Mohammed (pbuh) being the final Prophet Allah confirm His favours upon us and He is calling on all of mankind irrespective of race, religion,, ethnicity, or status of life, to follow the instructions and the guidance that He has laid down for all of us, and in this case specifically those of us who are involve in a marital relationship if we want to secure a blissful married life.

Marriage as an Institution

It is also very important that we all understand that the institution of marriage is not one of man's inventions, since its origin goes back to the Creator Himself who created Adam and created for him his wife and placed them both in the Garden, and the proof is as follows:

وَيَـٰٓـَٔادَمُ ٱسْكُنْ أَنتَ وَزَوْجُكَ ٱلْجَنَّةَ فَكُلَا مِنْ حَيْثُ شِئْتُمَا وَلَا تَقْرَبَا هَـٰذِهِ ٱلشَّجَرَةَ فَتَكُونَا مِنَ ٱلظَّـٰلِمِين

Adam! Dwell thou and thy wife in the Garden and enjoy (its good things) as ye wish but approach not this tree, or ye run into harm and transgression. (7/19)

So, in this verse of the Holy Quran, it is made clear that marriage is one of the divine institution that Allah Himself created and He is pleased with it, thus the Holy Prophet Muhammad (pbuh) informed us in an authentic Hadith in which he has stated; 'Marriage is part of my Sunnah, and he who diverts from it is not following me. Also, in another Hadith he (pbuh) tells us marriage completes half of our religion, so spend the other half in the worship of Allah.

Therefore, marriage has been enjoined upon the children of Adam (pbuh), as it was enjoined their father. It is only within the institution of marriage that the lawful reproduction of humans takes place in a manner that is pleasing to the Creator. The Almighty says.

وَمِنْ ءَايَـٰتِهِۦٓ أَنْ خَلَقَ لَكُم مِّنْ أَنفُسِكُمْ أَزْوَٰجًا لِّتَسْكُنُوٓا۟ إِلَيْهَا وَجَعَلَ بَيْنَكُم مَّوَدَّةً وَرَحْمَةً إِنَّ فِى ذَٰلِكَ لَـَٔايَـٰتٍ لِّقَوْمٍ يَتَفَكَّرُو

And among His Signs is He created for you mates from among yourselves, that ye may dwell in tranquillity with them, and He has put love and mercy between your (hearts): verily in that are Signs for those who reflect. (30/21)

Furthermore, in Islam marriage is considers to be a contract between a man and a woman in which rights and obligations are two of the most important fundamental pillars to be observed, and Allah has puts love and mercy as the two checks and balance at the disposal of the couple, and He conclude by reminding them to fear Him through whom they both claim their mutual rights. Allahu Akbar.

When this is understood and used in its proper context the couple will have a blissful life. For in times of trials and fitnah, when the Shaytaan causes the love to be lost, we will move to the other resort which is not violence and oppression, but that which Allah in His Supreme Wisdom has given them Rahman (mercy), and by resorting to the qualities of mercy love can once again be restored.

So marriage is not an institution in which violence, intimidation, and oppression, of either party becomes a way of life, but one in which by virtue of rights and obligation, cooperation and respect for each other both parties can enjoy a blissful life, guaranteed security for themselves, their children, other members of the family, and the society at large.

Walliship

The Walli is the father and guardian of his daughter. In a case where the parents of the man or the woman object to the marriage taking place between their respective children, and the couple has a reasonable basis for the marriage to take place against the wishes of their families, they can take the matter to the Islamic court, which has the power to decide in favour of both the man and the woman or the parent.

This principle is a corollary of the social directives of Islam and is corroborated by the following Hadith reported by in Tirmeedhi in Kitab al Nikah in which the Prophet (pbuh) said: A Nikah does not solemnise unless it takes place through the Walli, and, if someone does not have Walli, the ruler of the Muslims is the. In his article on Parental Consent in Marriage, Shehzad Saleem writes:

This Hadith is a corollary of the social directives of Islam pertaining to the institution of families and is based on great wisdom. Since the preservation and protection of the family set up is of paramount importance to Islam. It is but natural that each marriage takes place through the consent of the parents who are the foremost guardians.

It is also obvious that a marriage solemnised through the consent of the parent's shields and shelters the newly formed family for reasons already mentioned, and it is essential that the newly formed family be part of another larger family or the so-called extended family.

So from the evidence of the Hadith related by Aisha (rh) in which the Messenger of Allah said. If a woman marries without the consent of her guardian, the marriage is void. (Bulugh Al Maram) 836) Walliship is one of the most important pillars and a condition that have to be fulfilled for a marriage to be valid.

Who is the Walli?

Narrated by Abu Huraira that the Messenger of Allah said:

A woman may not give a woman in marriage, nor may she give herself in marriage. (Bullough AL – Marram 839) So, it is clear as stated in the Hadith of the Messenger of Allah (pbuh) that it is not permitted for a woman to give herself or someone else in marriage.

It is therefore logical that since she must be given in marriage by someone, that someone is called the walli and her first walli is her father. So, the false misconception that a woman can be given in marriage by her mother, her aunt, her sister or some female relative has not been derived from any revealed books of Allah, rather it has been derived from the vein desires of the innovators, therefore If this ever happens the marriage would be invalid.

So, the walli of any woman is her Muslim father and since in marriage the father relinquishes his responsibility of walliship to her, it becomes the duty and the right of the father to give his daughter in marriage to the man she will be marrying. When this is done the father surrender his responsibility as her walli to her husband who now becomes her walli. However, if a woman accepts Islam and her father has not, her father automatically loses the right to be her walli.

If the father of the girl is not qualified to be her walli because he is not a Muslim, then her Muslim uncle, or brother, or her son if she was previously married and has a Muslim son, who has reached puberty or the nearest Muslim male relative in her family may assume that responsibility. If none can be found it becomes the responsibility of the Muslim ruler as is apparent in the Hadith of the Messenger of Allah (pbuh) which is 'The marriage without walli is batil, batil.'

So, as for the revertees who has no male Muslim family them the Imam or a righteous elder, or the sheikh should be appointed for her as a wakeel, and through him proper investigations are made to ascertain all the relevant information that will insure making the correct decision whether she should proceed with the marriage, and Allah knows best.

Therefore, speaking as a Muslim, it has to be understood that contrary to the false claims and propaganda of the misguided and the misled, our women are regarded to us as the jewels in our crown, and she must be cared for and protected, therefore handing her care and responsibility over to another person, is something that has to be considered carefully, and Allah has put all the necessary checks and balances in place to ensure that this is done correctly.

Finding a Partner

The Muslim community is divided into different sections or groups. There are those Muslims who have studied Islam and stick to the Quran and the Sunnah of the Prophet Mohammed (pbuh).

There are also the Orientalises who have a system to themselves that has nothing to do with the Sunnah of the Prophet (pbuh). Then there are the traditionalists and the madhabbies, and all the other groups that falls within the category of the seventy-two sects that the Messenger of Allah (pbuh) has informed us about that are a stray.

There is also a section exclusive to the revertees to Islam who are trying to develop the correct system of recording prospective wives and husbands, where introductions can be made, which is a correct system that has been practiced by the people of the Sunnah for hundreds of years.

The Holy Prophet (pbuh) has given four points of reference which a Muslim man may use when seeking a wife, and these qualities are: beauty, wealth, piety, and he (pbuh) said piety is the best choice, but the criterion that is most prevalent today amongst brothers and sisters from the aforementioned groups is the one that is not mentioned by the Prophet (pbuh) and that is, ego. Ego is rife and being exploited at expense of ignoring the divine advice of the Prophet (pbuh).

This means that some of the brothers and sisters especially among the revertees are not taking the appropriate steps and measures to investigating the background of the sister or brother that he or she has met or been introduced to, then make their decisions based upon the advice of the Messenger of Allah (pbuh), after a thorough investigation preferable by their walli.

As an example, many are the times when marital problems arrive and we must deal with it, we find the sister, or the brother has not even met the families of their prospective spouse with a view of developing an assimilating possession with their extended families.

Neither have they done some investigation into the character or the history of their prospective partner to get an idea of the type of person they are about to commit themselves to. As a result of not following the proper protocol of patience and investigation, haste and ego has become the way that is followed, and therefore in too many instances regretfully, the result is divorce.

Allah has made a general statement to mankind who is hoping to get marry when courting a wife or a husband, and this is applicable to all people, irrespective of the time, place, nation, religion or tribe:

$$\text{ٱلْخَبِيثَاتُ لِلْخَبِيثِينَ وَٱلْخَبِيثُونَ لِلْخَبِيثَاتِ ۖ وَٱلطَّيِّبَاتُ لِلطَّيِّبِينَ وَٱلطَّيِّبُونَ لِلطَّيِّبَاتِ ۚ أُو۟لَٰٓئِكَ مُبَرَّءُونَ مِمَّا يَقُولُونَ ۖ لَهُم مَّغْفِرَةٌ وَرِزْقٌ كَرِيمٌ}$$

Women impure are for men impure, and men impure for women impure and women of purity are for men of purity, and men of purity are for women of purity: these are not affected by what people say: for them there is forgiveness and a provision honourable. (24/26)

Here Allah addresses an issue which is so prevalent among those who have chosen not to obey and follow the above Ayah's, and racially discriminate against pure innocent believers based on colour or cast. Any Muslims who behave in such a way towards other Muslims are no better than Iblis, the devout enemy of mankind, who refused to bow to Adam (pbuh) the father of humans, despite of Allah's command.

$$\text{قَالَ مَا مَنَعَكَ أَلَّا تَسْجُدَ إِذْ أَمَرْتُكَ ۖ قَالَ أَنَا۠ خَيْرٌ مِّنْهُ خَلَقْتَنِى مِن نَّارٍ وَخَلَقْتَهُۥ مِن طِينٍ}$$

"What prevented thee from bowing down when I commanded thee?" He said: "I am better than he: Thou didst create me from fire and him from clay." (7/12)

Muslim who rejects another Muslim for marriage based on ethnicity or tribal roots then he or she fallen into assabeya, racism as Iblis did saying he is better than Adam for the stated reasons. The Prophet (pbuh) warned: "He, who calls to assabeya, then let him bite on the penis of his father."

Allah does not discriminate against His slaves based on their ethnicity, which their parents are, or any other worldly matter. What matters on the scale of justice is piety; this is what Allah is looking at.

يَٰأَيُّهَا ٱلنَّاسُ إِنَّا خَلَقْنَٰكُم مِّن ذَكَرٍ وَأُنثَىٰ وَجَعَلْنَٰكُمْ شُعُوبًا وَقَبَآئِلَ لِتَعَارَفُوٓا۟ ۚ إِنَّ أَكْرَمَكُمْ عِندَ ٱللَّهِ أَتْقَىٰكُمْ ۚ إِنَّ ٱللَّهَ عَلِيمٌ خَبِيرٌ

Oh mankind! We created you from a single (pair) of a male and a female, and made you into nations and tribes, that ye may know each other (not that ye may despise (each other). Verily the most honoured of you in the sight of Allah is (he who is) the most righteous of you. And Allah has full knowledge and is well acquainted (with all things). (49/13)

I do not think I have to add any further comments with respect to who is the best among mankind since this verse of the Quran has clarified the issue past, present and future, for those who have

The Messenger of Allah (pbuh) said, "All of mankind has one father, "Adam", but different mothers. Allah had placed the total population of humans in the loins of Adam (pbuh) who begot his sons and passed on these genes to them, and they begot their children and passed on their successors to them. So, the cycle of reproduction of humans continues, and will continue until the Day of Judgment.

Consent

It is very importance that it is understood that although we are talking about consent between the prospective husband and wife that the consent and cooperation of their respective parents and families are also obtained.

The importance of this unity cannot be overstated, therefore it should be vigorously pursued to ensure their consent, for marriage does not only bring the wife and the husband together, but it is supposed to bring two families together.

With respect to the parents whose daughter has been sought in marriage it is important to note that in an authentic Hadith Narrated by Ibn Abbas (may

Allah be pleased with him) in which the Messenger of Allah (pbuh) said, "A woman who has been previously married has more right over her person than her guardian, and a virgin must be consulted, and her consent is her silence. (Bullough Al- Marram 838)

It is therefore of paramount importance that the consent of the girl's wail should be sought and his permission given for this marriage to be valid.

If the walli objects and his objection is based on un-Islamic reasons, such as assabeya, then the assistance of the Judge or the people of knowledge should be sought, who will give a ruling to determine the correct way forward Depending on the ruling from the people of knowledge one may or may not proceed with this marriage without the consent of the family.

In an ideal Islamic society, it is the parents who find a spouse for their son or daughter, but in a Jahilaya society in which we have different categories of Muslims such as Orphans, refugees without parents, widows, divorced women, and single parent, reverts from non-Muslim families one has to be very careful how these affairs are managed. These different social structures do sometimes present a problem that has to be dealt with tactfully, and in some cases the advice of the Ullamah should be sought to ascertain the correct method in dealing with them.

When there is no male Muslim in the i.e. father, brother, uncle, or son, the consensus of opinion of the people of knowledge is, that the sister must acquire a wakeel. This guardian should be a Muslim man, who is well respected in the Muslim community, the Imam or the Sheikh who is generally concerned for the welfare of these single women, and this wakeel or guardian should try and find a suitable husband for these respective women although it is allowed for previously married women to arrange their own affair or marriage, it is also required that they should be represented and given in marriage by a respected Muslim man.

Brothers and sisters should be aware that meeting each other without the supervision of a guardian is not allowed for Islam does not permit free mixing of the opposite sexes.

Therefore, all meetings between prospective husbands and wives should be chaperone even when consent for the marriage has been ascertained and this should continue until they are dually married. There are Islamic institutions and Masjids that have taken the responsibility of Walliship within their welfare department. So, it is advisable that brothers and sisters from non-Muslim parents seeking marriage should register themselves with them.

However, it is regrettable that the sisters are not sufficiently forthcoming to register themselves for marriage, and this has left a vacuum to be filled with respect to brothers who are Allah fearing and looking for wives?

Another problem is those Muslims who have discovered true Islam based upon the teachings of the Messenger of Allah (pbuh) with the correct understanding of the Salaf, and that is not what their parents have been practicing or teaching them. Saying this does not mean that it is wrong to follow a Fiqh Madthhab, but its following must be based upon the correct understanding and the guidance of the Ullamah.

Some of these examples are they only pray when they go to the masjid on Fridays, or on Eid days, or during the Holy month of Ramadan, or holding the view that marriages between Muslims can only take place within their own tribe, cast, or Madth-hab.

They advise their children that they should avoid Masjids that are integrated with nationals other than themselves or having a Madth-hab that is different from theirs. Once they have discovered that Islam is based on the teachings of the Book of Allah, and the Sunnah of the Prophet (pbuh) and according to the understanding of the rightly guided Salaf of this Ummah, the conflict within the family between traditional customs and the true teachings of Islam becomes apparent.

These new discoverers of true Islam amongst the sisters will want to choose a husband who has taqwah irrespective of his colour or cast, or because this man has got the correct Aqedah and Manhaj, and is able to maintain his family, and will be able, insha Allah, to save himself and his family from the fires of Jahannam.

To the misguided parents of these children, I can only ask them to look at the history of Islam, and they will see that it is by virtue of the legislation inherent in the revelation of the Holy Quran that the total abolition of the enslavement of women, and racism came about, and mankind was invited to let go, come away from, abandon, and forget the customs of the days of ignorance of our fathers who had no guidance. Allah advises the believers:

Allah stated in the Holy Quran states;

يَٰٓأَيُّهَا ٱلنَّاسُ إِنَّا خَلَقْنَٰكُم مِّن ذَكَرٍ وَأُنثَىٰ وَجَعَلْنَٰكُمْ شُعُوبًا وَقَبَآئِلَ لِتَعَارَفُوٓا۟ إِنَّ

We created you all from a male and a female, and made you into nations and tribes so that you may know one another. (and not to despise other) Verily the noblest of you in the sight of Allah is the most God-fearing of you. Surely Allah is All-Knowing, All-Aware. (49:13

كَيْفَ تَكْفُرُونَ بِٱللَّهِ وَكُنتُمْ أَمْوَٰتًا فَأَحْيَٰكُمْ ۖ ثُمَّ يُمِيتُكُمْ ثُمَّ يُحْيِيكُمْ ثُمَّ إِلَيْهِ تُرْجَعُونَ

O ye who believe! Enter Islam whole-heartedly; and follow not the footsteps of the evil one; for he is to you an avowed enemy (so give your children their rights, and fear Allah and die not except in the state of Islam). (2/208

Choosing a Husband

Choosing a husband can be summarized in the statement of Ali Ibn Thabit, may Allah be pleased with him, when a Bedouin Arab came to him to ask his advice in getting his daughter married. Ali said to the man "marry her to a man who has Taqwah." According to most of the major scholars Taqwah is describe as;

(a) Taqwah Al-khouf minal Jaleil. (To fear Allah.)

(b) Wall amalu bet-tanzeel.

To implement all the teachings of the Quran and the Sunnah of the Messenger of Allah (pbuh) with the correct understanding of the Salaf.

Wa istih daar yarma lika'a AR- Raheem.

To prepare ourselves for the day when we will meet.

Wa rida bil kaleel.

To be satisfied with whatever Allah has given us.

The man who brought his daughter to Ali (rh) Inquired why I should marry my daughter to this man who we do not know.

Ali rh. Said to him because "if he loves her, he will take care of her, and if he does not love her, he will not abuse her." So to here we have a truly clear understanding of the meaning of taqwah. Of course, the husband should be properly equipped to give his wife her rights which fall under the following headings.

Whereas the wife is the head of the home, the husband is the head of the family. This is based upon divine legislation under the rules of rights and obligation as it is the obligation of the husband to provide for his wife in terms of food, clothe and shelter, so he is the one who must go out in search of the means to provide for his family.

Secondly, he does not have to go through the regular monthly indisposition with its attendant adverse psychological effects, neither are his actions restricted by childbearing and giving birth, and the nursing of babies. In fact, it was Islam which delivered woman from been treated with contempt and been used as a chattel.

Rather Islam establishes her equality rights both theoretically and practically, by establishing her freedom of choice, and instituted laws which guaranteed her freedom of expression, inheritance and to be treated with dignity, instead of being treated with contempt.

In the chapter 16 v 58 of the Holy Quran Allah describe the way in which women were treated before the advent of Islam in the Arabian Peninsula. Here Allah described the attitudes, and evil talk of the men of those ages of darkness in the following statements.

ذَا بُشِّرَ أَحَدُهُم بِٱلْأُنثَىٰ ظَلَّ وَجْهُهُ مُسْوَدًّا وَهُوَ كَظِيمٌ (٥٨)

And when the news (of the birth of) a female (child) is brought to any of them, his face becomes dark, and he is filled with inward grief, so what does he do? HQ 16 V58)

يَتَوَارَىٰ مِنَ ٱلْقَوْمِ مِن سُوٓءِ مَا بُشِّرَ بِهِۦٓ ۚ أَيُمْسِكُهُۥ عَلَىٰ هُونٍ أَمْ يَدُسُّهُۥ فِى ٱلتُّرَابِ ۗ أَلَا سَآءَ مَا يَحْكُمُونَ

He hideth himself from the folk because of the evil of that whereof he hath had tidings, (asking himself): Shall he keep it in contempt or bury it beneath the dust. Verily evil is their judgment. (HQ 16 v59)

لِلَّذِينَ لَا يُؤْمِنُونَ بِٱلْءَاخِرَةِ مَثَلُ ٱلسَّوْءِ ۖ وَلِلَّهِ ٱلْمَثَلُ ٱلْأَعْلَىٰ ۚ وَهُوَ ٱلْعَزِيزُ ٱلْحَكِيمُ

For those who believe not in the Hereafter is an evil similitude, and Allah's is the Sublime Similitude. He is the Mighty, the Wise. (HQ16v60)

So we Muslims are proud to announce to the world that it was not the human or women rights of the Western World which came into existence yesterday that liberated women from the global oppression of vile men, rather it was through the legislation from Allah that Was revealed to the Prophet Mohammed (pbuh) addressing this issue and was enforcement by Law by the Prophet and his Companions that brought about the total liberation of the oppression, enslavement and disrespect of our mothers, sisters, daughters and wives globally.

Throughout the Holy Quran and the Sunnah of the Prophet (pbuh) the honour of women is being expounded to the extent where after believing in Allah as our Lord, the next allegiance in terms of is obedience is to our mothers, and when the Prophet (pbuh) was asked to explain He said, your mother, your mother three times before our father.

In inheritance her share is prescribed by Allah, as a wife the agreement to marry must come from her and not from the prospective husband, and whatever she brings to the marriage is hers, and whatever her husband has is for both, and Allah has further honour her by naming the fourth Surah (chapter) of the Holy Quran Nisa (English translation the Woman) and in this Surah the protected rights of the women is expounded in all walks of her life, from her childhood to old age. Whether it is marriage, divorce, inheritance, her rights of ownership, and her personal property etc., and here I would like to advise readers to take some time out and read chapter (4) of the holy Quran entitled An-Nisa' and capture its immense benefit.

It is also particularly important to note that in the process of the agreement which eventually leads up to a marriage contract it is the woman who Initiate the offer of marriage, a detail which emphasizes the bride's spontaneous freedom of choice in making this important decision.

I have concluded that I understand why some men especially in the West make false statements of how Muslim women are being oppressed by the religion of Islam, while the truth of the matter is, when they become aware of the rights of women in Islam, some of them they are afraid of losing the oppressive power they have held over women for the past eighteen hundred years, of which they are not prepared to give up.

But things are changing, and women are entering Islam faster than men, because they have that only the Truth can set them free, and the actions of a few misguided Muslims do not represent Islam Let us now set out to consider the obligations imposed by Allah upon the husband toward his wife, and then proceed to discuss her obligations toward her husband.

The Husband's Duties

يَٰٓأَيُّهَا ٱلَّذِينَ ءَامَنُوا۟ لَا يَحِلُّ لَكُمْ أَن تَرِثُوا۟ ٱلنِّسَآءَ كَرْهًا ۖ وَلَا تَعْضُلُوهُنَّ لِتَذْهَبُوا۟ بِبَعْضِ مَآ ءَاتَيْتُمُوهُنَّ إِلَّآ أَن يَأْتِينَ بِفَٰحِشَةٍ مُّبَيِّنَةٍ ۚ وَعَاشِرُوهُنَّ بِٱلْمَعْرُوفِ ۚ فَإِن كَرِهْتُمُوهُنَّ فَعَسَىٰٓ أَن تَكْرَهُوا۟ شَيْـًٔا وَيَجْعَلَ ٱللَّهُ فِيهِ خَيْرًا كَثِيرًا

O ye who believe! Ye are forbidden to inherit women against their will, neither should ye treat them with harshness, that ye may take away part of the dower ye have given them,-except where they have been guilty of open lewdness; on the contrary live won a footing of kindness and equity. If ye take a dislike to them it may be that ye dislike a thing, and Allah brings about through it a great deal of good. H.Q. (4/19)

The Messenger of Allah (pbuh) in an authentic Hadith says:

"Fear Allah, fear Allah in the matter of women. They are your weak partners, a trust from Allah with you; and they are made by the divine word permissible for you."

Immolating the examples of the Prophet the husband should be loving and relax with his wife while making agreeable gestures to her. It further recommended that a husband should be relaxed with his wife and cheer her up with his humour or by making agreeable gestures. The Prophet, (pbuh) despite his lofty, used to compete with his wife Aisha 'may Allah be please with her,' in athletic race, sometimes she won, and other times he won.

The Prophet (pbuh) addressing his companions used to say, "Surely, Allah does not love a rough person who is boastful, and rude to his wife. A husband is responsible for the protection/security, happiness, and maintenance of his wife. Although she may have to cook, he must buy her the raw materials and provide her with the cooking and kitchen facilities, as may be required and applicable. He is also obligated to buy her suitable clothing that corresponds to the season of the year. or one that matches the climate in which they live.

However, the number of sets of clothes and their quality will depend on the husband's means and social requirements. A wife is also entitled to a comfortable, independent accommodation, suitably furnished, and provided with basic sanitation facilities.

If the necessity arises, she is obliged to stay with the husband's parents or relatives, but he is not obliged to live with hers. It is also her wright to relax with her husband in an atmosphere, free from the embarrassment caused by the presence of another adult in the home.

In addition to providing these necessities, he is not and should not provide her with any forbidden substances. He should be kind, understanding and forgiving, and he must treat his wife in a tender and loving manner. He should avoid hurting her and should bear with her if she ever does something disagreeable, so long as this act of mercy does not spoil her, and she is not persistent in her bad behaviour. Addressing his issue Allah stated in the holy Quran.

يَٰٓأَيُّهَا ٱلَّذِينَ ءَامَنُوا۟ لَا يَحِلُّ لَكُمْ أَن تَرِثُوا۟ ٱلنِّسَآءَ كَرْهًا

O you who believe you are forbidden to inherit women against their will, and you should not treat them with harshness. (HQ 4 v19)

And the Prophet (pbuh), says: Fear Allah, in the matter of women. They are your weak partners, a trust from Allah with you; and they are made by the divine word permissible to you. He also said, "Whoever, of you whose wife behaves in a disagreeable manner and he responds by kindness and patience, Allah will give him rewards". That being the case patience behaviour was the practice of the Prophet (pbuh), even when any of his wives dared to address him harshly.

Once the Prophet's mother-in-law saw her daughter Ayesha (rh) strikes the Prophet (PBUH) with her fist on his noble chest. She became so enraged that she began to reproach her daughter. The Prophet (pbuh) smilingly said, "Leave her alone; they do worse than that."

On another occasion Abu Bakr, the Prophet's father-in-law, was invited to settle some misunderstanding between him and Aisha (rh). The Prophet (pbuh) said to her, "Will you speak, or shall I speak?" Aisha (RA) said, "You speak, but do not say except the truth. Her father "Abu Bakr (rh) was so outraged that he immediately struck her severely, forcing her to run and seek protection behind the back of the Prophet (pbuh). Abu Bakr (rh) said to her, "O you the enemy of herself! Does the Messenger of Allah say but the truth?"

In response the Prophet (pbuh) said, "O Abu Bakr, we did not invite you here for this harsh dealing of (rh), nor did we anticipate it.

It is further recommended that a husband be relaxed with his wife and cheer her up with his humour or by making agreeable jokes. On one occasion the Prophet heard an Abyssinian entertainment team playing outside the home, so the Prophet (pbuh) said to his wife Aisha (rh), "Would you like to see them?" When she agreed, he sent for them and they came and performed in front of his door.

The Prophet (pbuh) stretched his hand, putting his palm on the open door and letting Aisha's (RA) chin rest on his arm so that she could see comfortably. A while later the Prophet (pbuh) asked Aisha (rh) Enough but she remain silent. After while he asked, "Enough?" and the answer was again, "Silence!" But when he asked her for the third time Enough She agreed, "Yes," and the team went away on a gesture from the Prophet (pbuh).

It must be said that the importance of love and mercy between the husband and the wife, the Ullamah have taken great interest in explaining the importance of love play, and the techniques that arouse excitement, between the couple. The Islamic literature dealing with this subject is far more original and stimulating than the crude and vulgar exhibition of pawn that is widely been circulated today in the co called modern world.

It is the consensus of the scholars especially the early ones who were, and still specialised in the field of marital relationship emphasized the importance of love play, fondling, kissing, and romantic expressions in order to arouse the wife's sexual passion and prepare her for a deeper sensation and a successful conclusion.

The Prophet of Islam (pbuh said, "the most perfect believers are those who are best mannered and most tender with their wives. He (pbuh) also said, "Surely Allah does not love a rough person who is boastful, and rude to his wife." A Bedouin widow once described her husband: "He came always with a smile and left with a greeting. When he was hungry, he ate whatever was found, and was not bothered when something was missing!"

Sexual Etiquettes

It is of paramount importance that the husband should handle the sex relationship between himself and his wife with the utmost care, gentleness and understanding. He should not regard his wife as an object for his own enjoyment and pleasure, but as a partner with whom he seeks mutual happiness, satisfaction and fulfilment, so his approach to her should always be described as loving, gentle, and tender.

The newly married couple must exercise a certain degree of respect and caution, in dealing with each other, and the husband must be very gentle as it related to sex especially if his wife is a virgin. This will be her first experience of been with a man who she may have only met for short period, she is going to be shy and to a certain degree nervous.

It is therefore the husband's responsibility to exercise patience and make sure she is in a state of relaxation and comfort, and when the actual act of intimacy takes place, he should endeavour to ensure that she reaches a full degree of satisfaction. As Muslims we recognise the intimate relation between a husband and his wife is a Sadaqah for which the husband and the wife will be rewarded by Allah, and that the Shaytaan is ever coming between a man and his wife, therefore before any sexual relation commences the appropriate dowah should be offered to Allah which is as follows "Allah'huma ageniba shaitan, wageniba shaitan maa razk tana"

In the name of Almighty Allah, Oh Allah wards off the evil forces away from us and from the blessings you bestow upon us. It is highly recommended that there should be foreplay between the husband and his wife in order to stimulate their sexual desires which will contribute to a more complete fulfilment. As human beans Muslims or non-Muslims (taharah) purification from impurities forms an essential part of our daily lives, therefore after sexual relation it becomes necessary to perform the required ablution that may be required. As for the Muslim complete (ghusl) bath must be performed before certain acts of worship is offered like Salat, reading the Quran, and any other act of worship that is legislated in the sharia.

Love makers may exclaim their feelings during love making but should be careful that such expressions do not disturb the privacy of the act itself. Some Companions of the Prophet (pbuh) recommend the repetition of the words: Allahu Akbar, "Allah is the Greatest."

On the other hand, it is to be remembered that the liquid (lubricating) material discharged by the sex organs on excitement is counted as pollution and a polluting element in Islam; therefore, it is forbidden for Muslims to smear parts of his or her body with this polluting stuff unnecessarily.

It also to be understood that oral sex in forbidden in Islam. We also believe that this act is indeed disgusting; and this disgust might in the long run plant the seeds of hatred in the hearts of the couple and ultimately break their relationship. The mouth was created to speak, eat, recite the Holy Quran, praise, glorify, and zikr Allah, and therefore it should not be used to consume haram substances, or to indulge in anything that is najas.

Although the position to be assumed by the male and female during sexual intercourse have had a great deal of attention by Muslim scholars who are specialist in this field of research suggested around fifteen basic different positions.

However, whatever position the couple find attractive, suitable, and comfortable for themselves should be their choice. It is highly recommended that the husband should endeavour to achieve mutual orgasm with his wife, and if he should fail to hold out sufficiently for his wife, he should continue his efforts to have her reach a climax as to rush away from her too soon might be injurious.

It is said variety is the spice of life, therefore it is highly recommended that the husband should change his romantic approach to his wife and sexual performance, even in small details, as these changes could intensify the pleasure, excitement and enjoyment in your relationship.

The correct approach to love making is summarised in the Hadith of the Prophet (pbuh) when he said, let not one of you fall upon his woman in the manner as a male animal suddenly jumps over its female victim. Let there be a message between them". He was asked, "What is the message, O Messenger of Allah?" He replied, "Kissing and endearing speech".

In another Hadith it was related that he said: Three practices are shortcomings in a man; namely:

To fail to inquire about the name of a man he has just encountered but was worthy of friendship.

1. To refuse a favour extended to him in good faith
2. To assault his woman without introductory entertainment i.e.:

To stimulate her only for him to satisfies his own desire before she can achieve her own fulfilment. The Messenger mentioned, "when one of you retires with his wife, let them not strip off their clothes completely in an animal-like manner; and let him begin by stimulating her by the use of fine exciting speech and kissing". In the process of love play the husband and his wife may enjoy and fondle any part of the body of each other; as their engagement in this kind of activity is regarded as a type of divine devotion.

Sexual relationship is strictly forbidden during the menstrual period of a woman, and penetration in the back passage is always forbidden. Prohibition also applies to all types of unnatural and unproductive activities, whether committed between two persons of the same sex or not.

The matter of frequency coitus should be left to the mood and the personal inclination of the parties concerned, which indeed depend on many factors, including their age and the condition of their health. A husband should also see to it that his wife has sufficient knowledge of her religious obligations and encourage her in observing her devotional duties.

Special attention will have to be given to the prohibition of sexual relationship not only during the menstrual cycle but also during the period of postnatal discharge which comes after childbirth, as during these periods the obligatory mandatory prayer is lifted until the bleeding is completely stopped, then ghusl has to be performed, then normal relationship and prayer be resumed. A husband should not harbour doubts or undue suspicion about his wife although Jealousy is a natural attribute given by Allah, but it should be used wisely. The husband is responsible to protect his wife against corruptive influences but spying and suspicion should not be the method through which he becomes watchful and judgemental upon his wife.

The Prophet (pbuh) said:

There is a type of jealousy which Allah loves and there is another type which He hates. As for that, which Allah loves, it is the jealousy which is provoked by a legitimate cause of suspicion; and that which He hates is the jealousy which is unduly aroused". The Prophet (pbuh) once asked Fatimah (ra), his own daughter, "What is best for a woman?" She replied, "That she should not mix with men and men should not mix with her." The Prophet (pbuh) who was pleased with her answer hugged her and said, "An offspring resembling its roots.

Therefore. in order or the family to remain upon goodness neither the husband nor the wife should not behave in a manner that will draw suspicion to him or her. Children becomes a natural result of mutual cooperation between the husband and the wife, and Allah has described in the Quran the state of affairs as it reflects the treatment of the wife by the husband during the duration of pregnancy, childbirth, and after the child is. He has also legislated the responsibilities, and mutual rights of decision making of both the husband and the wife regarding the upbringing of the children.

وَٱلْوَٰلِدَٰتُ يُرْضِعْنَ أَوْلَٰدَهُنَّ حَوْلَيْنِ كَامِلَيْنِ ۖ لِمَنْ أَرَادَ أَن يُتِمَّ ٱلرَّضَاعَةَ ۚ وَعَلَى ٱلْمَوْلُودِ لَهُ رِزْقُهُنَّ وَكِسْوَتُهُنَّ بِٱلْمَعْرُوفِ ۚ لَا تُكَلَّفُ نَفْسٌ إِلَّا وُسْعَهَا ۚ لَا تُضَآرَّ وَٰلِدَةٌ بِوَلَدِهَا وَلَا مَوْلُودٌ لَّهُ بِوَلَدِهِ ۚ وَعَلَى ٱلْوَارِثِ مِثْلُ ذَٰلِكَ ۗ فَإِنْ أَرَادَا فِصَالًا عَن تَرَاضٍ مِّنْهُمَا وَتَشَاوُرٍ فَلَا جُنَاحَ عَلَيْهِمَا ۗ وَإِنْ أَرَدتُّمْ أَن تَسْتَرْضِعُوٓا۟ أَوْلَٰدَكُمْ فَلَا جُنَاحَ عَلَيْكُمْ إِذَا سَلَّمْتُم مَّآ ءَاتَيْتُم بِٱلْمَعْرُوفِ ۗ وَٱتَّقُوا۟ ٱللَّهَ وَٱعْلَمُوٓا۟ أَنَّ ٱللَّهَ بِمَا تَعْمَلُونَ بَصِيرٌ

Mothers shall suckle their children for two whole years; (that is) for those who wish to complete the suckling. The duty of feeding and clothing nursing mothers in a seemly manner is upon the father of the child. No-one should be charged beyond his capacity. A mother should not be made to suffer because of her child, nor should he to whom the child is born (be made to suffer) because of his child. And on the (father's) heir is incumbent the like of that (which was incumbent on the father). If they desire to wean the child by mutual consent and (after) consultation, it is no sin for them, and if ye wish to give your children out to nurse, it is no sin for you, provide that ye pay what is due from you in kindness. Observe your duty to Allah and know that Allah is Seer of what you do. HQ. 2 v233.

If the wife becomes pregnant, her husband should display a greater level of care for her, and he should do all he can to alleviate her discomfort. When she is delivered, he should be grateful to Allah for her safety and for what Allah has beneficently graced them with. If his wife has delivered a male child, he should not go out of his way to show his pleasure; and if it is a female, he should not at all feel disheartened; after all he does not know which is better for him.

The Prophet (pbuh) said whoever is graced with a daughter and treats her well and lavished on her, it will be a protection for him against the punishment of the hell fire, and he should be grateful for the favours that Allah has bestowed upon him. Whoever brings home some good things to his children, it will be counted as a divine charity for him.

Let begin by giving the female ones. Whoever cheers up a female child shall have the merit of him who weeps out of divine fear of Allah and whoever so intensely fears Allah, Allah will protect him from the hell fire.

The Messenger of Allah (pbuh) said whoever has two daughters or two sisters under his care and treats them well, he will be my companion in Paradise. A child, however, should be given a good name, even if it is delivered in a miscarriage. And shortly after a child's safe birth, the full text of the call to prayer should be recited in its right ear, and the short one in its left ear.

It is recommended that a boy be circumcised on the seventh day of his birth, excluding the day of birth itself. Whether it is a boy or a girl, it is recommended that the family then hold a feast for which a lamb or larger animal should be sacrificed. Some of the meat should be distributed to the poor, as well as the value of gold whose weight is the weight of the baby's hair. The sacrifice offered on the seventh day of birth is known as 'Aqedah.

At this point I do not think I should add any further comments on this subject as the legislation in the Quran and the Sunnah should be sufficient for those who fear Allah and the last day.

The Wife's Duties

Since the wife is the head of the home it is her responsibility to create a clean and comfortable house where she and her husband can have a peaceful and relaxing environment, if the husband provides her with the necessary means for her to do that. It is also her to prepare the food, and make sure that the home and family cloth wear is kept clean, and whether these tasks are done by her or it is done by an employee, it should be done under her supervision.

A wife must be faithful and devoted to her husband. Her loyalty is due to him first, even before her parent, and she should not associate with other men who are none marham for her or people who could bring harm to the family. Although the responsibility of the wife is to ensure the proper running of the home, this does not mean that the husband should just sit back and expect to be served by his wife as if she was the slave of the family. He should be ready to give a helping hand whenever the occasion present itself, especially when the family begin to increase, and the wife has added responsibility of looking after the child or children.

Of course, this will depend on what he can do, and what is to be considered here is that by giving a helping hand it will not only alleviate the workload of the wife, but it will increase the love and respect she has or him, as well as setting a good example for the children.

I have deliberately extended the above passage in order to emphasize and explain the rights of women in a marital relation due to my concern that I have develop over the years through my professional experiences of workings a married counsellor and trying to find solution to a verity of dysfunctional marriages, and having seen the grief expressed by many women, and listening to their complaints regarding the constant abuse of our daughters and sisters who have had the unfortunate experience of becoming battered wives.

It has become apparent to me that a lot of men especially young men of today do not understand how a woman really function, and they want to get married, but they do not take the time and opportunity that is available to them to learn how to manage their marital affairs in a positive Islamic way through patience, understanding, and tolerance, when dealing with marital disputes, instead of becoming intolerant, aggressive, and argumentative leading to physical confrontation.

On the other hand, our sisters should learn to respect their husband and be careful of their language and the choice of words they are using to express themselves to their husbands

During my research of writing and putting this book together I came across what I can only describe as one of the best and most beneficial advice that could ever been given by any parent to their daughter with the sole intention of preparing her to become a wife.

So, I take great pleasure in sharing it with my readers. I would also like to and mention that no one can claim the ownership of this advice except the lady who offered it hundreds of years ago, as the Prophet has stated 'aDeenan nacea' the religion is an advice.

Advice to all women

It is related that an ancient Arab Lady who had a wealth of experience as a wife and a mother decided to advise her daughter on the eve of her wedding day as follows:

O my daughter! You are leaving the home in which you were brought up to a house unknown to you and to a companion unfamiliar to you.

Be a floor to him, he will be a roof to you; be a soft seat to him, he will be a pillar for you; and be like a slave girl to him, he will be like a slave boy to you.

Avoid inopportune behaviour, lest he should be bored with you; and be not aloof lest he should become indifferent to you.

If he approaches you, come running to him; and if he turns away, do not impose yourself upon him.

Take care of his nose, his eye and his ear. Let him not smell except a good odour from you; let his eye not see you except in an agreeable appearance; and let him hear nothing from you except nice, fine words. In managing the household, you should economize and avoid extravagance. You should not give away your husband's wealth except within the degree of his approval.

Whatever you give within this degree, you will share in its divine reward; and what you give away beyond it will be to the advantage of your husband and to your own disadvantage on the Day of Judgment.

Conclusion

In the forgoing passages derived from The Book and the Sunnah and the of the Ullamah I have tried to outline and explain some of the mutual rights and obligations of a husband and the wife as set out and stipulated by Islam for the guidance of its adherents, reveals the following facts: The husband-wife relationship is to be based not on dry legal rules or decisions of the court but on mutual respect, love, mutual co-operation and regard for each other. The husband is alone responsible for the entire cost of her upkeep, and the wife is the mistress of the household.

The objective of each is to serve the other and to provide for each other an environment of comfort, enjoyment and happiness; with an aim of achieving optimum bliss for each other, while setting a good example for their offspring which will be preserved as a lasting benefit for humanity. A woman is not a chattel or a blind follower but an equal partner.

It has to be emphasised that her soft nature, and her natural role as the partner who is to provide more for the sexual attraction and excitement, her monthly menstrual discharge with its attending psychological and physical adverse effects, and her childbearing and being a mother have made her not only dependent, but a respected, virtuous, and beloved partner.

Within this framework and mutual considerations, and within the Islamic flexibility which has regard for custom, prevailing traditions, which are consistent with the moral values of Islam, the couple may choose any type of arrangement for the distribution of their mutual responsibilities in order to meet their needs as they may see fit in the conditions prevailing where they live.

An interesting point which should be emphasized is that the wife does not lose her own independent character on getting married because she retains her full maiden's name. So, Miss Malika Amin on her marriage to Mr Yusuf Ali is still called Malika Amin and not Malika Ali. So, she may be referred to as Malika's wife of Mr Ali but not plain Malika Ali This right that is given to women under Islamic Law establishes her independence and freedom for her continued relation with her own family.

Cultural Perception of Marriage among Muslims

Preparing the Children for the Next generation.

وَٱللَّهُ جَعَلَ لَكُم مِّنْ أَنفُسِكُمْ أَزْوَٰجًا وَجَعَلَ لَكُم مِّنْ أَزْوَٰجِكُم بَنِينَ وَحَفَدَةً وَرَزَقَكُم مِّنَ ٱلطَّيِّبَـٰتِ ۚ أَفَبِٱلْبَـٰطِلِ يُؤْمِنُونَ وَبِنِعْمَتِ ٱللَّهِ هُمْ يَكْفُرُونَ

And Allah has made for you Azwaj (mates or wives) of your own ki, and has made for you, from your wives, sons and grandsons, and has bestowed on you good provision. Do they then believe in false deities and deny the Favour of Allah? (HQ.16V72)

This is clear proof that Allah has placed sexual urge in humankind as a means by which the procreation and continuity of the humanity is ensured. Sex is indeed a strong driving force in the human being which demands fulfilment. Islam recognizes this urge and never denies it but regulates it through the institution of marriage. Just as Islam strictly forbids sex outside marriage and anything leading to it, it also prohibits celibacy.

In a Hadith related by Abdullah bin Mas'ud (rh) (Bulugh AlMaram 824) In which the Prophet (pbuh) said, "Young men, those of you who can support a wife should marry, for it keeps you from looking at women and preserves your chastity.

Therefore, a young man who is physically and financially capable to marry should be encouraged to do so as early as possible. The parents of a young woman who is ready for marriage should let her marry as soon as an acceptable man proposes to her.

Just as they have been warned about the dangers of fornication, the young people should know the many benefits of marriage. Besides being a lawful way of satisfying one's sexual urge, marriage is considered a form of worship, and the sexual act itself is a (Sadaqah) good deed for which the Muslim will be rewarded as is proven in the following Hadith of the Messenger of Allah (pbuh)

Related by Abu Huraira, rh) that the Prophet (pbuh) said.

"And in the sexual act with your spouse there is a charity, and you will be rewarded for it. He was then asked: "A man satisfies his urge and gets reward for it? He said, he get reward for it" Then he said: "Do you see if he satisfied it in an unlawful way, would he not get a punishment?" They said: "Yes," and then he said: "Similarly if he did it in a lawful way, he will be rewarded for it. (Related by Muslim) Through marriage, men and women find tranquillity and peace with each other. Allah (pbuh) says:

$$\text{وَمِنْ ءَايَٰتِهِۦٓ أَنْ خَلَقَ لَكُم مِّنْ أَنفُسِكُمْ أَزْوَٰجًا لِّتَسْكُنُوٓاْ إِلَيْهَا وَجَعَلَ بَيْنَكُم مَّوَدَّةً وَرَحْمَةً ۚ إِنَّ فِى ذَٰلِكَ لَءَايَٰتٍ لِّقَوْمٍ يَتَفَكَّرُونَ}$$

And among His Signs is this, that He created for you wives from among yourselves, that you may find repose in them, and He has put between affection and mercy. Verily, in that are indeed signs for a people who reflect HQ 30V21

Marriage ensures the halal growth and spread of the Muslim Ummah. It splits the responsibilities of raising the child between the wife and the husband and the extended family and tightens the bond between the generations. When young people become aware of the many benefits of marriage, they will no doubt look forward to it.

It is the responsibility the parent to choose a spouse for their children, and to educate them about the etiquette of betrothal. They should also inform them about the lawful and the unlawful, the likes and dislikes, the permitted and the prohibited from an Islamic point of view on their wedding night and beyond.

Relationship outside Marriage

A lot have been said regarding the excellence of the marital relationship and the great blessings and reward from Allah to those who have taken up this responsibility

All the major scriptures including the Toro, the Ingil, and the Quran have borne witness to this lawful human relationship between men and women known as marriage that was instituted by Allah (God) himself.

The opposite of this is described in the following words such as Adultery, and this description applies to the people who are already married, even if they are divorce and fornication apply to those people in this relationship who never been married but cohabiting.

s for the none Muslims who are involved in this type of what can only be described as an unlawful relationship, I am not here to be judgemental upon you, but because I wish you what I wish for myself, if you are fortunate enough to read this book, then I advise you the pay strict attention to the following verses of the Holy Quran and save yourself from the fire, because the Lawful and the Unlawful relationship between man and women is also mentioned in the Bible and the Toro, and the Quran being the last Testament is a reminder of what has being revealed before by God.

As for the Muslims who are involved in this haram practice, I advise you to Fear Allah and amend your ways before it's too late.

Allah said. In the Holy Quran.

وَٱلَّذِينَ لَا يَدْعُونَ مَعَ ٱللَّهِ إِلَٰهًا ءَاخَرَ وَلَا يَقْتُلُونَ ٱلنَّفْسَ ٱلَّتِى حَرَّمَ ٱللَّهُ إِلَّا بِٱلْحَقِّ وَلَا يَزْنُونَ ۚ وَمَن يَفْعَلْ ذَٰلِكَ يَلْقَ أَثَامًا يُضَٰعَفْ لَهُ ٱلْعَذَابُ يَوْمَ ٱلْقِيَٰمَةِ وَيَخْلُدْ فِيهِۦ مُهَانًا إِلَّا مَن تَابَ وَءَامَنَ وَعَمِلَ عَمَلًا صَٰلِحًا فَأُو۟لَٰٓئِكَ يُبَدِّلُ ٱللَّهُ سَيِّـَٔاتِهِمْ حَسَنَٰتٍ ۗ وَكَانَ ٱللَّهُ غَفُورًا رَّحِيمًا

And those who cry not unto any other god along with Allah, nor take the life which Allah hath forbidden save in (course of) justice, nor commit adultery-and who so ever doeth this shall pay the penalty.

Their torment will be doubled for them on the Day of Resurrection, and they will abide therein disdained forever. Save those who repent and believeth and doth righteous work; as for such, Allah will change their evil deeds to good deeds. Allah is ever Forgiving, Merciful. And whosoever repents and doeth good, they verily repent toward Allah with true repentance. (HQ25V68,69,&70)

I think this is sufficient as an admonition and an advice for those Muslims who have gone astray but still believe in Allah and the last day, to examine themselves and return to the path that is straight. Allah seratual Mustakeem...

As for the non-Muslims it is also a wakeup call to follow the Scripture that you claim to be following and since we are all believers in the Day of Judgment, and on that Day either the Priest or the blood of Jesus will not save you from the punishment of disobeying.

Although this book is intended to be about Marriage however, I have decided to include a chapter on Divorce which includes some case study I did for two main reasons.

The first reason is because currently divorce is extremely prevalent among marriage couples, and the second is, within the Islamic community which is my main concern divorce seems to be taken for granted, and in a lot of cases the proper procedures are not followed.

So hopefully through this research I hope to bring a better understanding of its disadvantage, and the awareness that although divorce is lawful, it is one of the most hated things in the sight of Allah, and finally to be sufficiently educated to understand the Fiqh of divorce.

Therefore, we men should fear Allah and the last day in the way we handle the affairs of marriage and divorce, for we will all stand before Allah and account for our word and actions, and being the shepherd of our families in this life. Also the women should fear Allah in relation to their obligations to her husband.

May Allah protect from the evil consequences of divorce and preserve or Marriage. Ameen.

Talaaq / Divorce

The Arabic word Talaq (divorce) means to set free, and according to the Sharia, Talaq is to free the woman from the bond of marriage.

In a Hadith narrated by Ibn. Maajah (2081) in which the Messenger of Allah (pbuh) said.

Talaq is for the one who seizes the leg. (i.e. Consummates the marriage'. i.e., Classed as Hassan by al- Albaani in Irwa al-Ghaleel, 2041).

That being the case divorce becomes the right of the husband and does not take place unless it is done by him. Based upon this understanding, the scholars of Islam said if a man is forced to divorce his wife by Talaq wrongfully, and divorces her under pressure, then the divorce is not valid.

(See al-Mughni 2041).

The author of this book is giving a warning to those families who are ordering their son in laws to divorce their wives, 'In the language of 'set my daughter free' for some un-Islamic reason as has become prevalent in some societies. I say to you Fear Allah and remember that you will meet and give account to Allah for the harm you have caused in destroying a legitimate marriage.

The woman can also seek divorce, which is known as Kula, but if she should seek divorce from her a husband for non-legitimate reason and gets it, even if it is through a court of man made law and she goes through her Iddah and then she gets married to another man, she would be committing adultery for the fact that she would still be married to her so- called divorced husband.

When our Shaykh Muhammad ibn Saleh al Uthamyeen (RA) was asked about a similar matter his response was;

Some good and righteous people should get involved to bring about reconciliation between the husband and his wife. Otherwise, she will have to give him some payment so it will be a proper Shariah Chula.

So, what the sheikh is indicating here is if the wife seeks Kula after reconciliation has failed, she will have to return the mahr to her husband that she was paid by him when they got married, and that would release her from the ties of the marriage

So once again let us remind ourselves of the divine statement of the Messenger of Allah (pbuh) in the Hadith related by Ibn Omar (rh) in which he stated that the Messenger of Allah (pbuh) said, "The lawful thing which Allah hates most is divorce". (Bullough Al Mahram 915)

From this we come to understand that divorce is among the legal things which is halal, but it is not always the best solution to marital problems because of the negative and disadvantageous effect it has on the family.

However sometimes situation the between the husband and the wife become too problematic to be resolved, then in that case divorce becomes the only solution to a relationship that has become unsustainable.

On the other hand, on many occasions divorce become a cause of enmity and disunity in the family, which sometimes lead to very destructive consequences including unlawful deaths which is the delight Iblis the accursed devil and the enemy of mankind.

Some reasons for Divorce

The reasons for divorce can vary according to circumstances affecting the family. Some of the legitimate reasons are as follows:

1. The most serious of all is apostasy; one of the couples has apostates from Islam.
2. Proven adultery or fornication.
3. The woman was married before but did not tell her present husband.
4. Immoral and un-Islamic behaviour from the spouse.
5. The husband or wife lies about their drug or alcoholic addiction before marriage.
6. Impotence of the husband and cruelty towards one's wife or husband.
7. Refusing to support one's wife.
8. Being unable to have congenial relations.
9. One who lies about their lineage?

In the above Hadith the Messenger of Allah (pbuh) said, "Divorcé is for the one who seizes the leg".

This Hadith clearly give the husband the rights of divorce.

Today all over the world conferences and conventions are held, and poisonous voices have been raised propagating depraved opinions regarding the ethic and principles upon which marriage and divorce should be based.

One of these ruling is to restrict the right of the husband in pronouncing divorce ineffectual unless it is done in a court, in the presence a judge.

However, from the above Hadith and the Shariah point of view, divorce is the right of the husband and not the right of any judge.

So, my first advice is to the sisters who will only accept divorce if it is done in a court be it a Shariah or civil court, is to follow the laws of Islam through which you got married, and do not become confused by non-Islamic laws, except if there are other legal matters of which the husband and wife cannot agree upon, or if you had a secular marriage.

In that case in order to achieve a so-called legal separation one will have to go to a secular court. A typical example is, you are living in a country where Islamic marriages are not recognised or upheld by the host government, and the couple had a secular marriage i.e., you were married in a register office. So, to have that marriage dissolved one must go through a civil court and file for a divorce.

A Judge will then examine the case presented by both parties and if in his judgement this marriage is not reconcilable, he may grant the couple what is known as a Dicer Nice, and within a period the marriage will be terminated.

My second advice is for the brothers who think word Talaq can be inserted in every little dispute between you and your wife, and it becomes binding without going through the process of advice, arbitration with a view to bring about reconciliation is a complete misnomer. So, unless these processes are followed you will be doing a great harm to yourself and.

Also, it must be understood that for a Talaq to be valid it must not be pronounced in a state of anger, either by saying Talaq two or three times in one sitting constitute absolute divorce. However, if it was not done in a state of anger it is regarded is one Talaq.

Finally, if three Talaq were pronounced over a period, whether it is three months, six months, and one or ten years, you would be irrevocably divorced, and your wife is no more halal for you unless certain conditions are fulfilled namely

فَإِن طَلَّقَهَا فَلَا تَحِلُّ لَهُۥ مِنۢ بَعْدُ حَتَّىٰ تَنكِحَ زَوْجًا غَيْرَهُۥ ۗ فَإِن طَلَّقَهَا فَلَا جُنَاحَ عَلَيْهِمَآ أَن يَتَرَاجَعَآ إِن ظَنَّآ أَن يُقِيمَا حُدُودَ ٱللَّهِ ۗ وَتِلْكَ حُدُودُ ٱللَّهِ يُبَيِّنُهَا لِقَوْمٍ يَعْلَمُونَ

And if he hath divorced her (the third time), then she is not lawful unto him thereafter until she hath wedded another husband. Then if he (the other husband) divorces her it is no sin for that they come together again if they consider that they can observe the limits of Allah. These are the limits of Allah. He manifested them for people who have knowledge. (HQ 2/230)

So once again my advice to the brothers is to fear Allah, learn your Deen, and be serious about the institution of marriage, and do not treat the Legislation of the Shariah of Islam as a joke, but call to mind the words of the one who Allah has favoured with the honour of revealing the Quran, for he (pbuh) has highlightened and exemplified the importance of the institution of marriage as one of the greatest institutions in the Deen of Islam, and the method and conditions of entrance into, and exit from a marriage contract has been clearly defined and explained in the Book and the Sunnah.

Taken from the verse of the Holy Quran in Surah Al Baqarah,

وَٱنظُرْ إِلَى ٱلْعِظَامِ كَيْفَ نُنشِزُهَا ثُمَّ نَكْسُوهَا لَحْمًا ۚ فَلَمَّا تَبَيَّنَ لَهُ قَالَ أَعْلَمُ أَنَّ ٱللَّهَ عَلَىٰ كُلِّ شَيْءٍ قَدِيرٌ ۚ

And look at the bones [of this donkey] how We raise them and then We cover them with flesh. And when it became clear to him, he said, I know that Allah is over all things competent" (2:259)

In this verse of the Holy Quran, the Arabic word "Nushooz" is used which is translated as 'to rise or it rose.' So basically, it implies something that is raised or elevated. From this comes the word "Naashiz" implying that a vein is bulging or protruding.

The husband commits "Nushooz" to his wife by treating her harshly, and wrongly raising himself above her due to his hatred of her.

The disobedient wife is called "Naashiz" because her behaviour is one of rising and elevating herself above the position of obeying her husband.

So, from this the scholars of Islam have concluded that the word Nushooz is the legal term that describes whatever the cause may be that ultimately leads to divorce.

If we take some time to research the word Nashaza in lexicon we will find that it is used in different senses, and also has a number of meanings, so eventually one will conclude that the word Nushooz is most fitting to describe the great fitnah that leads to divorce.

When one looks at the different meanings and context in which this word is used, we discover that its usage varies according to the occasions and context amplifying the different senses describing negative behaviour.

This choice of word leaves one pondering over the supreme wisdom of Allah (Hickmah to Baligah) in choosing such a word that fits so many purposes. Some of the meanings are as follows:

Trying to raise one, or elevate oneself, rising or elevating

Refusal, no longer obeying, refractoriness, harm, hatred, anger, disagreeing with, differing from, leaving another, not fulfilling another's rights, coldness, causing discomfort, scorn, contempt aversion, haughtiness, distancing, to be averse and disinclined, straying away from proper behaviour. When we look at the legal definitions of the jurists, and the Ullamah we find that Nushooz on behalf of the wife revolve around any of the following characteristics.

Bad manners or the wife refuses to fulfil her obligations that Allah has imposed upon her towards her husband.

She does not beautify herself for her husband when he desires that from her.

She disobeys her husband with respect to coming to his bed, and she refuse to respond to his call.

She leaves the house without his permission or without any legal right to do so.

She does not perform the obligatory religious duties such as failure to perform the prayers, fasting in Ramadan, performing pilgrimage, and any other obligatory acts of worship in Islam,

As for the husband Nushooz has also four characteristics:

The husband wrongfully elevating and rising himself haughtily above his wife.

He transgresses her by beating her, harming her, reviling her, abusing and cursing her.

Not treating her properly and intentionally willing to harm her.

Refusing to maintain her with respect to her food, drink, clothing, or boycotting her in the bed etc.

In general, Nushooz combine both speech and action.

I could continue to give evidence, rulings, and advice from the Book, the Sunnah and the scholars, which is very necessary and beneficial for the correct or proper guidance and understanding of handling marital affairs, however since the purpose of this exercise is to deal with divorce, let me conclude with some of the rulings based upon the consensus of the Ullamah.

Arbitration

Arbitration has been sanctioned in Islam to stop wrongdoings, stop dispute, prevent disorder, suppress oppression, argumentation, and to enjoin and order the good, and eradicate evil. So, arbitration between spouses is permissible when the use of other means fails. If all the efforts that Allah permits have been applied in a marital dispute, for example admonition, boycotting, beating and all other reasonable attempts have been made to bring back the two together have failed, arbitration becomes the final resort to try and restore affection,

وَإِنْ خِفْتُمْ شِقَاقَ بَيْنِهِمَا فَٱبْعَثُوا۟ حَكَمًا مِّنْ أَهْلِهِۦ وَحَكَمًا مِّنْ أَهْلِهَآ إِن يُرِيدَآ إِصْلَٰحًا يُوَفِّقِ ٱللَّهُ بَيْنَهُمَآ ۗ إِنَّ ٱللَّهَ كَانَ عَلِيمًا خَبِيرًا

And if ye fear a breach between them twain (the man and wife), appoint an arbiter from his folk and an arbiter from her folk. If they desire amendment Allah will make them of one mind. Lo! Allah is ever Knower, Aware. (HQ 4/35)

Based upon this verse of the Holy Quran in which Allah has stated that, "if you fear a breach between them appoint two arbiters etc."

The scholars of Islam have agreed that two arbitrators should be appointed if the two spouses are not able to come to agreement between themselves and separation is looming, or dissension occurs between them, and it is not known which of the two spouses is committing Nushooz.

Two arbitrators should also be appointed if both spouses are committing Nushooz and the husband refuse to keep his wife, then the arbitrators have a very significant and important role to play, as well as having a noble and virtuous responsibility in bringing about rectification, Islaah and restoring love and harmony to a disunited family.

This is a praiseworthy role that is loved by Allah and He has promise to reward it in the following verse.

ا لَّ خَيْرَ فِى كَثِيرٍ مِّن نَّجْوَىٰهُمْ إِلَّا مَنْ أَمَرَ بِصَدَقَةٍ أَوْ مَعْرُوفٍ أَوْ إِصْلَـٰحٍۭ بَيْنَ ٱلنَّاسِ ۚ وَمَن يَفْعَلْ ذَٰلِكَ ٱبْتِغَآءَ مَرْضَاتِ ٱللَّهِ فَسَوْفَ نُؤْتِيهِ أَجْرًا عَظِيمًا

There is no good in much of their secret conferences save (in) him who enjoined almsgiving and kindness and peace-making among the people. Whosoever doeth that, seeking the good pleasure of Allah, We shall bestow on him a vast reward. (HQ. 4/114)

Making Islaah between the spouses does not only benefit the married couple but it benefits the complete family and the community.

There is a difference of opinion among the scholars concerning the authority or the right of the arbitrators as to whether they have the right to separate the couple. One opinion is that they are simple agents for the spouse therefore they can only do so with the permission of the spouses, for their role is only to bring about reconciliation and nothing else.

The other opinion is that they are appointed by the judge or the ruler to solve a problem. They are therefore like judges and the judge can decide according to what is in the best interest to solve the marital problems, regardless of if that act of best interest is either reconciliation or separation. According to the great imam Ibn Al Qayyum Al Jowziyya (ra) who said.

Allah has given them the position as arbitrators and not trustees (wakeel) and is working on behalf of the spouses, therefore they are judges who has the authority to separate or bring about reconciliation between the newly wedded wife and her husband before or after the marriage has been consummated for judgement has been put in their hands.

Finally, the word arbitration lexically means to judge or decide. In the Arabic language one says (bakkamatal rajul) meaning when a matter has been given over to him to decide, and in this case, it is the arbitrators who decide.

Based upon this and other opinions of major scholars, arbitrators have the right to decide and act in the best interest of the spouses whether it is reconciliation or separation. Ultimately there are only three legal and lawful ways of acquiring divorce. (1) The husband pronounces Talaq (1) The wife seeks a Kula. The arbitrators make a judgement of divorcing the couple and Allah knows best.

The question has been asked what if the husband to divorce his wife before he consummates the marriage

- Divorce before Consummation.

    Cultural Perception of Marriage among Muslims

Addressing this issue Allah says in the Holy Quran.

وَإِن طَلَّقْتُمُوهُنَّ مِن قَبْلِ أَن تَمَسُّوهُنَّ وَقَدْ فَرَضْتُمْ لَهُنَّ فَرِيضَةً فَنِصْفُ مَا فَرَضْتُمْ إِلَّا أَن يَعْفُونَ أَوْ يَعْفُوَ الَّذِي بِيَدِهِ عُقْدَةُ النِّكَاحِ وَأَن تَعْفُوا أَقْرَبُ لِلتَّقْوَىٰ وَلَا تَنسَوُا الْفَضْلَ بَيْنَكُمْ إِنَّ اللَّهَ بِمَا تَعْمَلُونَ بَصِيرٌ

If you divorce them before ye have touched them (have had sexual relationship with them) and you have appointed unto them a portion, then (pay the) half of that which ye appointed, unless they (the women agree to forgo it, or he agrees to forgo it in whose hand is the marriage tie. To forgo is nearer to piety. And forget not kindness among yourselves. Allah is Seer of what ye do. I.e. Half of the mahr that you have agreed upon. (HQ 2:237)

Our noble Shaykh Ibn Uthaymeen (May Allah have mercy upon him). Commenting on this verse, he said even if he was alone with her, but did not have intercourse with her, the same ruling applies, and she is entitled to a half. Most of the scholars are of the same opinion concerning this issue.

It has been narrated that there was a consensus among the companions of the Prophet (pbuh) (may Allah be pleased with them, that if he had been alone with her, then she is entitled to the whole mahr. They regarded being alone with her is like intercourse.

Explaining the correct understanding of the itchti-had of the companions, Imam Ahmad (ra) said that it was possible for him; the husband to do with her what was not possible for anyone else to do. Sharh al-Mumti,' 5/326).

So, based upon the speech of Allah, the understanding of the Companions of the Messenger of Allah (pbuh) and the consensus of the scholars, we have the correct answer to this very important question.

Although there are two answers to the same question, it must be understood that both answers are correct.

Allah stated that if the marriage has not been consummated then the wife is only entitled to half of the mahr. However, the correct understanding of this ruling has to be that of the Companions.

Therefore, from a Fiqh point of view, there is a distinct difference between the husband who has been alone with his wife and then decides to divorce her, and the husband who was not alone with her.

So, it is regarded that the husband who has been alone with his wife, had access to her to do whatever he wanted, which is also his right, as opposed to the husband who had no access to her either by choice or otherwise.

So, her entitlement would depend upon what took place after the marriage in terms of access or being alone with her or not, and Allah knows best.

Finally, both the husband and the wife have mutual rights whether a half of the mahr is paid, or it is paid in full or waved. For Allah has given the right to the husband to pay half, or the full amount which is nearest to piety, and He has also given the wife right to forgo it, and Allah is Merciful and Wise.

In conclusion I ask Allah our Creator and Protector Who has given us this wonderful institution of marriage in which humans is reproduced in a halal way to protect us from the deception of Iblis the accurst devil and his adherents. Ameen.

O Allah, I am grateful to you for your favours that you have bestowed upon the Ummah of Muhammad (pbuh) and I ask you to protect us from the evil of Shaytaan and his ascribing partners unto You yaa Ahad yaa Samad, and I seek refuge in You Yaa Allah from Iblis and his aiding and abetting the husbands and wives in bringing Nushooz into their marriage lives. Ameen.

The Effects of Divorce on the Family

In the compilation of this book, I think it would be of some benefit to those husbands and wives who may be contemplating divorce without seriously thinking about the destructive consequence this action could have on their families to pay strict attention to the experiences of those couples who have been through this process.

So, to address this issue I have decided to include some case studies I did with a few divorce couples who have gone through the process of divorce, perchance some lessons may be learnt from their experience. Let me begin by saying there is a quote which goes something like this "A wise man/woman learns from the experiences of others". So, I hope perhaps some lessons may be learnt from the experiences of those who have gone through the fitnah of divorce.

Before I bring you up to date with the trauma of divorce, I would like to share with you an especially important observation of mine having dealt with quite a few divorce cases. It is my experience that In a lot of divorce cases, the governing principle of making the decisions to divorce are always based upon two things, emotion and anger, and what comes after is the reality of its effects which can only be dealt with rationally.

Therefore, my advice is that one should think hard of what they are about to do by getting divorced, and question themselves as to whether or not they have sincerely made the efforts to find solutions to rectify the on-going problem or problems before embarking upon breaking this sacred union, destroying something that our Creator loves only to replace it with something that He hates.

I am not saying divorce is not allowed, but nevertheless it is something that Allah hates. Think about It; My final advice is all Muslim married couple should read verses (221 to 242 of surah to Baqarah to have a basic understanding of marriage and divorce, and Allah's help we seek.

Case Study 1

Mrs Abdullah,

I have decided that all the participants who were kind enough to take part in this research will remain an anonymous; therefore, they will be referred to as Mr. And Mrs Abdullah. Or H &W husband and wife as the case may allow. Also Q. Stands for question or an A. stands for answer.

Having drafted the relevant questions to the subject, she agreed to have the interview in the comfort of her home.

Accompanied by my son my first question to her was.

(Q) How and when did you meet your husband?

(A) In 1992 having lived in London for some time I returned to the Land of my birth to visit my mother. It was while I was staying there with my mother the sister of my now divorced husband came to spend some time with my mother, and this was customary during the summer season, friends and families would visit each other and spend some time together.

(Q) So, it was while his sister was at your mother's home the formal introduction was made?

(A) Yes.

(Q) How did things develop and at what point you both decided to get married?

(A) I returned to London after a short holiday, and we corresponded for a while and then he travelled and we lost contact for about a year and then he contacted me again and soon after that I returned to the Caribbean to take this on-going discussion further regarding what we both want to do and it was during this period we agreed to get married.

(Q) Did you get married during this visit?

(A) Yes, it was during this visit to the Caribbean we both agreed to get married, so we went to see the Imam at the Masjid having agreed on a date, and we had an Islamic Marriage.

After a few weeks I return to London, then about five or six months later he joined me here where we had a secular or Register Office marriage.

(Q) Now you are both married and living together, was it difficult to make the necessary adjustment in coming to terms with each other's difference?

(A) No. There were not any difficulties, we both came from a similar cultural background and most of our aspirations were similar in terms of what we wanted out of life in professionally and otherwise so, this helps to shape our mutual agreement in many areas of our living together.

(Q) Two of the greatest fundamental assets on which the stability of a marriage depends are rights and obligations. These two great fundamental assets are not manmade laws but are legislation that is found in the Shariah of Allah as the two basic foundations upon which the stability of the marriage is based. Then we are commanded to 'Fear Allah through whom we claim our mutual rights

Meaning these rights and obligations are not manmade laws but are the legislations laid down by Allah. So the rights of the wife become the obligations of the husband, and the rights of the husband become the obligations of the wife.

Having said that and you have affirmed its understanding, so my next question is.

(Q) Were these rights and obligations met or upheld by both of you during the marriage?

(A) Yes, except for the fact that when my husband arrived in the United Kingdom for the first five to six months he did not work and that was not a problem as I did not want him to work, because he had no legal status to do so.

He had some money, and I was working so between us we took care of some of the expenses of living until his papers were sorted out and his situation changed then he began to work and he took care of his side of his responsibilities to the best of his ability so I had no complaints, and of course I believe I also gave him his rights.

Mash-Allah.

(Q) Were there happy or good times during the marriage, and if so, would you like to name a few?

(A) Yes of course there were good times especially in the beginning of the marriage there were good times. We were newly married, we were incredibly happy, even when my first child was born, we were very, very happy we had the same outlook. So things were very good in the beginning of the marriage, but I think as the marriage progresses problems began to arrive.

(Q) Were there any children produced from the marriage and if so, what are their age and their sex?

(A) Yes, there are three children, two girls and one boy. The two girls are thirteen and fifteen, and the boy is eight years old.

(Q) Are they living with you or their dad, and what are they doing?

(A) Yes, they all live with me, and they are all going to school.

(Q) And what about visiting rights for the dad?

(A) The dad comes on a Sunday and he spends the day with them. However, at the moment the oldest girl does not want to see her Dad, so it's only the two younger ones that he spends Sunday with. He also comes around during the week to visit the children and make sure they are all alright.

(Q) What is the reason or whose fault is it that has brought about this strange or bad relation between the dad and his oldest daughter?

(A) I would say it is the daughter's and not the father's fault. However, I believe the father should sit down with his daughter and explain certain things to her. Maybe because he thinks she cannot get through to her he has giving up trying.

Never lest, I think this is a mistake on the father's side, for even though she may say she do not want to talk to her father, he has got to make the efforts to sort this out, for by leaving her to come to terms with herself will only encourage her to continue with this unacceptable behaviour.

Therefore, I think this is the wrong approach from the dad in solving this problem.

Because in marriage it is not just the wife and husband that comes together,

Cultural Perception of Marriage among Muslims

it is also the families of both the husband and the wife that are joined together as a family, hence my next question.

(Q) What was the nature of the relation between you, and you are in laws like?

(A) Although not all his family were living in the U.K. generally, we had a very good relationship, as we would be in contact regular by the phone or other means, and of course there were the occasional visits.

(Q) What was it, and at what point of the marriage did things begin to change for the worst?

(A) After about two years' little cracks begin to occur in the marriage but they were sorted out and we continue to have a good relation.

(Q) Do you want to elaborate on these or are they personal and you would like to leave it?

There were times when problems would come up, but we did not understand them. For example, there was a time when he was not working and I was working so I would come in from work and I would be tired, but he could not accept or understand that, so for him it should be business as usual.

(Q) How were these problems rectified, did you call in the family, or the in-laws to try and find a solution?

(A) No not so much the in laws but we would go to the Masjid and speak to someone of knowledge, and he would help us to resolve to problems.

(Q) So at what point of the marriage in terms of time and action did things reach a level where you begin to see divorce as the only option left for both of you to have a peaceful settlement?

(A) This happened when he decided to take a second wife, but even after that the marriage was still going for another four years, although sometimes we found ourselves going in different directions. We wanted different things, also he had someone else to care about, and I had no one else to care about except our family and that put a strain on our relationship.

(Q) Did you feel that as a result of this new relationship with him having a second wife your rights were withheld or taken away from you?

(A) Yes. Things had changed, and I felt that my rights were not given to me.

(Q) Were there periods of separations and reconciliation before divorce became the final option?

(A) We both travelled to Africa to have a look around to see if there was a possibility of making the Hijrah there, and it was while we were there that he decided to take another wife. I was shocked by this experience based upon the age difference and his change in attitude towards me.

After his marriage to the new wife, things began to change so much. I became very unhappy, so I decided to return to the UK and that was our first separation, but before I returned to the UK, I told him I wanted a divorce

However, after a while he came back to the UK and we resolved some of the issues and we went back together.

After that we stayed together for a few years and then the marriage broke down again, and for me it was the last straw, and I did not want any reconciliation.

(Q) So now you both agree to separate, how did you both proceed with the divorce?

(A) I asked him for a divorce and to make it easy, he pronounced Talaq, and we are now going through the court of the land in the UK to have the marriage legally annulled.

(Q) Was there any final settlement in terms of assets?

(A) No we both agreed that the children should stay with me and he has his visiting rights, and we are both happy with that.

(Q) Do you have any regrets?

(A) No with exception that the children especially the boy who misses his father very much, but generally all the children would prefer if both parents were together. As for me now, I have a lot of responsibilities. I am doing an Open University course in Social Studies, I am also taking care of my extremely sick mother who had a stroke, plus she has demeanour.

I have also got to take care of the children getting them to school and the madrasa to improve and develop their Islamic development, plus the usual motherly care and responsibilities.

Then there are also the social aspects of the children's life which we must cater for such as sports, football games and other social functions to improve their development generally, so at the moment I am fully occupied which leaves me little time to contemplate regrets.

(Q) Where do you want to go from here with your life, what are your plans for your future?

(A) Well as I said before, now I am doing an Open University Health and Social course with the intention Insha-Allah if I can do a degree and that is one of my main plans for the future.

(Q) How old is your youngest child?

(A) She is eight years.

(Q) It will be another ten years before your youngest daughter reaches the legal age of responsibility, and by virtue of your aspirations and your plans I would assume since you are still a young lady permit me to put this question to you Do you intend to live the rest of your life as a single mum or do you intend to get married again?

Another point I would also like to raise before you answer this question is, based upon my general experience in this field without attributing any disrespect to you directly or indirectly is.

I have found in many cases whenever unfortunately divorce becomes the final solution to problems in a marriage to couples who have reached middle ages say late thirties early forties, they seem to reconcile themselves just to look after the children, without thinking that these children are going to grow up one day. Maybe they either get married and settle down with their own responsibilities or remain single but they have gone their separate way.

Considering that we do not live in a society where the extended family is a part of our culture who we can depend on in times of necessities. They are also immensely helpful in terms of support and assistance to divorce families in times of need,

What is the reason that it has become so prevalently among middle aged women that after divorce a large percentage of them choose to live alone with the usual TV or radio for their company instead of finding another partner and get on with living a reasonable life based upon partnership?

(Q) 'Don't you think you have some rights left and the fact that because one marriage has failed does not necessary mean that marriage is a failure, for history has shown that companionship of the opposite sex is a natural way to preserve a happy and reasonable life for the human race.'?

(A) Yes, I agree with what you are saying, and I have not got the answer to the choice that is been made by other women, but at this moment and time of my life the way I feel, I am quite happy looking after my children, taking care of my mother, and getting on with my studies.

(Q) My final question to you is, if an offer of marriage were to come to you now, what would be your reply?

(A) My reply would be no, because of the complications it would bring to the family, plus when you have gone through a recent divorce, to become involved in another marriage so early it would have a very bad effect on the children. However maybe in the distant future it could be considered.

(Q) Jazaakum Allahu Khorana. Thank you for your contribution to this research, and I hope that those who are privileged to read this narrative of yours may get some benefit from your shared experience.

Case Study 2

Mr. Abdullah

So I will proceed in the like manner of posing the same questions to this brother as I posed to his ex-wife.

(Q) How did you meet your wife?

(A) I met in 1992 in the Caribbean when we were both non-Muslims and she came from the UK to visit her mother. My sister was also visiting her mother and my sister made the interdiction. She returned to England shortly after, but we kept in touch.

It was during that period some eighteen months later that I became a Muslim, while she was also in the process of becoming a Muslim. Some months later she also became a Muslim in the UK and returned to the Caribbean for another visit, and it was at that point we decided to get married.

(Q) How and where did you get married? Was it an Islamic marriage or a secular marriage?

(A) About two weeks after she arrived in the Caribbean, we went to the Masjid to see the Imam and after consultation with him he advised us to get married, and we had an Islamic marriage.

(Q) So, what happened after the marriage?

(A) She returned to the UK and seven months later I came and join her, soon after which we decided to have a secular marriage in the register office.

(Q) How long did it take you both to come to terms with your differences and to make the necessary adjustments to complement each other's differences, and was the adjustment difficult before you settled down as a peace-loving couple?

(A) Things started out alright but after a while I began to realise that it was becoming difficult for my wife to accept and abide by certain rules and regulations which Islam requires from us, which was mainly to do with her obedience to her required obligations as a wife.

I think because she has been a very independent person, and now to have someone else in her life was becoming difficult for her, in terms having to give up some of the freedom that she once had, and now she had to answer to her husband in some cases, was something she was finding difficult to accept.

(Q) Did she eventually begin to obey and fall in line with what was required or expected of her?

(A) Yes, she fell in line only to a certain extent, but not in a lot of required cases.

(Q) Did you and your wife take in consideration that you had two different marriages; one was to do with the legal system of the land in which you both lived, and from the other comes the Islamic requirements which is based upon the legislations in the Quran and the Sunnah of the Prophet (pbuh) which forms the ethos or the foundation upon which the whole marital relationship is based?

Among these legislations are the requirements of rights and obligations, and only when these obligations are met, the life of both husband and wife will function based on Taqwah?

Inherent also in these legislations are the conditions upon which mutual agreement and tolerance are based, which helps to make the relationship between the husband and the wife acceptable and compatible

(Q) Did you both understand these Islamic principles and try to put them into practice?

(A) Yes but only to a certain extent but we manage to get there somehow, for in those early days of our marriage we did not have much knowledge of Islam, so we started attending Islamic circles, and classes while making the necessary efforts not only to learn but to implement what we understood from these classes within the household.

That contributed a lot to a better understanding of Aqedah and Manhaj, and what was required or expected of us in terms of (as you say) rights and obligations to be fulfilled as a husband and as a wife.

Nevertheless, it was still difficult for my wife to come to terms and obey some of the requirements that she had to fulfil.

As for me I have always maintained my family, and I do not think my wife has ever had any complaints about her maintenance except when I travelled to Africa.

(Q) What about when you just arrive in the country, could you afford to fulfil those financial obligations?

(A) To a certain extent yes because I did not arrive empty handed, but for about six months I was not allowed to work so for a short while I was short of money, but after that period I began to work, and I was able to take care of my obligations.

(Q) Were there times of happiness during the marriage?

(A) Yes, there were many good times when we were incredibly happy as a family

For example, we used to travel frequently.

We went on Umrah to Saudi Arabia, we went to Egypt, and Morocco, and we used to go for long drives with the whole family visiting different parts of the country, picnicking, so we used to enjoy ourselves as a family in many ways.

However, I must say many of the good times that we had were based upon me not putting too much pressure on my wife by demanding my rights, instead I compromised and gave up some of my rights in order to have a reasonable peaceful life, for she found it difficult in some cases to be obedient to some of the obligations she had to fulfil.

(Q) Were there any children from the marriage, if so, what are their sexes, and how old are they?

(A) Yes, there are three children two girls and one boy. The oldest girl is fifteen, the second daughter is thirteen, and the boy is eight years old.

(Q) Were you happy to be a father?

(A) Well, I am a family man, I have always wanted to have a family to have a wife and children is something I feel very strongly about, so yes, I was very happy.

Cultural Perception of Marriage among Muslims

(Q) How would you describe the relationship between you and you're in laws? Excellent, good, not too bad, could be better, bad?

Because from an Islamic point of view marriage does not only join a man and his wife together, but it is supposed to bring two families together.

(A) Excellent. My wife and I have our mother, father, brothers, sisters, cousins, nephews, mother and father in laws, uncles and aunts, and even today although my wife and I are divorced we all still have a particularly good relationship.

(Q) We are now arriving at a stage in this interview which we could call the crux of the matter. For I would hope that the experience of both your wife and you during the process of the marriage and divorce that you are both sharing with us may be of some benefit to other married or prospective married couples.

Hopefully, they will read my book and if they are facing marital difficulties, through your shared experiences they may find some amicable solutions to address their problems. For it is said that a wise person learns from the experiences of others.

So, my next question is:

(Q) At what stage or period of the marriage did the relationship became so strained that you or your wife, or both of you began to find life so unbearable that you saw divorce as the only solution to your problems?

(A) Several things happened throughout the marriage which makes me very unhappy, but the most significant was the disobedience of my wife and that stayed in the relationship for an exceptionally long time.

There were times when I was really stressed because of her disobedience in terms of upholding, or not honouring my rights, but as I said, for a peaceful life I would compromise on things that really annoyed or bothered me.

It reached a stage where things became so bad that I began to have negative feelings that we were not going to be together much longer because I cannot bring myself to accept her behaviour any longer.

It was at that point I began to think that it would not be wise for us to have any more children.

There were immense problems relating to bedroom issues, lack of cooperation to the extent where I ended up having to see the doctor and being put on medication which I did not take. Eventually I had counselling, and that helped me to deal with it physiologically, and even after that I still exercised patience hoping some changes are going to come.

(Q) Was your wife aware of what was going on and was it as a result of her behaviour that brought on your physiological, emotional, and physical problem?

(A) Yes, she knew but to be honest I do not think she cared. As for her problem I have never found out what really was the cause.

(Q) Were there any efforts made by both of you to rectify the situation?

(A) Yes. We used to have lengthy discussions, sometimes we would be up late at night until two in the morning trying to find solutions to her problem without success, and Allah bears witness that I tried to preserve my marriage.

It reached a point that I thought if I should take another wife that would help, but when I suggested it to her, she made a big fuss that she was never going to accept it. Eventually we went to see one of the Imams in the Masjid to get some advice and having listened to both of us he advised me to cancel the idea of taking a second wife for the time being.

So, I did as he advised just to please her, hoping by doing so it would bring about the changes I was hoping for.

It was soon after this that I decided to go to Africa to see if there was the possibility of making Hijrah, and while I was there, I was introduced to a very good family.

Among them was a very respectful young lady who was also looking for a husband and although our ages were different and I was already married she had no problems being my second wife, so with her family's agreement I got married to her and she has remained as my devoted wife ever since.

(Q) Masha-Allah. Having listened to your side of the problem in your marriage, it is not often that I do this, but I think there could be some benefits if I elaborate a bit about an incident that took place between the Messenger of Allah (pbuh) and one of his wives whose name was Sawda bint Zama.

The Prophet (pbuh) decided to divorce this wife based upon some deficiency that he found in her. So, he informed her of his decision and the reason why he had to that conclusion. Having informed her, she did not become angry and begins to accuse the Prophet (PBUH) of being unreasonable, selfish or unfair. She looked at the reasons why her husband has chosen to divorce her and concluded that what the Prophet said about her was the truth.

So, what was her reaction? She decided which was based upon justice. She (May Allah be pleased with her offered to give the time that the Prophet (pbuh) used to spend with her to another one of his wives as a compromise with the condition that the Prophet (pbuh) should retain her as one of his wives.

As a result of her wise offer, the Prophet (pbuh) accepted her offer as a compromise without divorcing her, and today she still retains one of the highest positions any woman could achieve in this life of being a wife of a Prophet which will continue in the hereafter, and of course also being one of the mothers of the believers. This principle is left as a Sunnah for this Ummah to follow if we only have sense.

In this true story lays one of the greatest examples of amicable solutions to marital conflicts based upon justice, rights and obligations, being fair and rational. So married partners should accept their own deficiencies and come to reasonable solutions within the framework of what is allowed in the religion, rather than using divorce as the first stop as solution to intolerance and disagreements within the marriage.

This is one of the noblest examples left for us Muslims by the Prophet of Islam (pbuh and one of his wives and mother of the believers, that should be follow tenaciously for reasons of its inherent benefits of preserving our marriage and solidifying the family structure.

Surely this Sunnah must be revived and brought back to life for it does not only save and guarantee the honour and preservation of marriage and the family, but it also adds light and stability to this sacred relation by us respecting and upholding the rights, care, and showing mercy to each other, while upholding the commandment of Allah "Fear Allah through whom you demand your mutual rights".

For this is one of the verses that the Messenger of Allah (pbuh) chooses to recite in the marriage ceremony known as Khutbatul Haajah reminding both the husband and the wife of the commandment of Allah which should be obeyed, and in which lies great benefit.

If there should arrive a situation in a marriage whereby because of some form of illness, whether physical or physiological, or other than these, one of the parties becomes incapable of fulfilling his or her obligations, we must ask ourselves this question, how are we supposed to deal with it. Are we going to seek a divorce, walk out of the marriage, neglect our partner, or are we going to resort to patience, care, love and mercy?

To address this question, let us look at the verse of the Quran in which Allah tells us,

$$\text{وَمِنْ ءَايَٰتِهِۦٓ أَنْ خَلَقَ لَكُم مِّنْ أَنفُسِكُمْ أَزْوَٰجًا لِّتَسْكُنُوٓا۟ إِلَيْهَا وَجَعَلَ بَيْنَكُم مَّوَدَّةً وَرَحْمَةً ۚ إِنَّ فِى ذَٰلِكَ لَءَايَٰتٍ لِّقَوْمٍ يَتَفَكَّرُونَ}$$

"And from among His Signs is that He created for you mates from among yourselves, who ye may dwell in tranquillity with them. He has put love and mercy between your hearts. Verily in that are Signs for those who reflect" (30:21)

Furthermore, in the case where the problem causes the wife to be incapable of fulfilling her husband's rights, is it right that she should rebel if her husband chooses to take a second wife while he still retains and maintain her? This is the question which must be answered by some, if not all Muslim women if they fear Allah and the Last Day.

(Q) So, at the request of your wife, you pronounced Talaq to her over the prescribed period then after her edat you separated.

(A) Yes.

It is also my understanding that you had a secular marriage, and if that was the case you will have to go through the secular court to have that aspect of the marriage annulled.

Whenever a sister asks her husband for a divorce, he should not just say

Talaq to her to make the process easy for her without first ascertaining that the reason for her request is justified from an Islamic point of view. If you are not sure, then consult the people of Knowledge for advice to see if her request is valid according to the Shariah. Certainly, if you give her Talaq and her request is invalid you would be helping her to commit a sin which has serious Islamic consequences.

If you have checked it out and her claim is invalid, you should advise her to fear Allah, and if she insists then leave her to take her complaint to the Shariah court but do not give her Talaq.

(Q) What is the relationship between you and your children?

(A) Well as I said we had three children and the last two are awfully close to me but my eldest is very distant from me.

(Q) Why is this?

(A) It started some time ago when I would admonish her, and she would become angry and complain to her mother. However instead of agreeing with me for trying to correct our daughter's bad ways, she would tell her your dad is always harsh with us. This has caused our daughter to develop certain attitudes of resentment towards me, and not wanting to aggravate the situation I have chosen to leave it alone.

(Q) Have you ever asked anyone to intercede or advise her that what she is doing is wrong and that she will be questioned and maybe punished by Allah for her ill manners to her parent?

(A) Yes, I have asked an Imam to speak to her, and after speaking to her told me it would be better if I leave it for a while and just keep being nice to her and in time she may begin to change. However, recently when I visit the children as I normally do, she came over from the neighbour's house and greeted me and we spoke briefly.

When I was leaving, I went and say salaams to her and she replied, so I hope gradually she will begin to see the error of her ways and some changes will begin to appear in her behaviour towards me.

(Q) Do you have any regrets about this separation?

(A) No, none except for my children who I know would like for me to be home with them, and that is a shared feeling between us.

(Q) Have there been any settlement between your wife, and you based upon valuables or jointly held assets?

(A) We have signed an agreement to that effect.

(Q) My next question is, now that you are divorced where you do want to go from here, and what are your plans for your future? Although you have stated that you have no regrets regarding the divorce, I believe there must be some form of remorse, surely you didn't get marry just to get divorce?

(A) Two things really. Now I am living here in the UK alone and my other family is in the Gambia, so I would like to get my family over here for I need to be here for the next foreseeable future.

Secondly, I could get another wife, but now I think I will put a hold on that. However, if the feelings should come back to me again, I may think about it seriously.

(Q) We will now turn to the final question. What advice would you like to give to both men and women whether married, or single, or contemplating marriage?

(A) First to the brothers who are contemplating marriage, I advise you to pay strict attention to the sister's knowledge of Islam and her willingness to learn and implement Islam in her daily life. For only when the husband and the wife are having a relationship that is based upon the principles of the Islamic code of conduct, they will begin to enjoy their marriage.

For without having mutual respect and fulfilling each other's rights and obligations as legislated in the Shariah, they will never be protected from the Shaytaan the accurst devout enemy of mankind.

Furthermore, in times of problems which we seek refuge in Allah from, it is only through sound knowledge of the Deen, solutions will be accessed. So I advise my brothers and sisters to seek knowledge, for Islamic knowledge is the only weapon that will defeat the Shaytaan.

Secondly, if you are caught up into a non-Muslim family relationship, and there are some marital problems, quite often the family has no rational unbiased suggestions to offer. So, my advice will always be to marry sisters whose family have an Islamic background, or the non-Muslim family respect the religion of Islam

However, if she is a sister who comes from a Muslim family, you should insure she is serious about her Deen, she is going to classes to try and understand the religion, she is learning the Quran and the Sunnah, learning Arabic, learning Fiqh etc. in other words she is striving to become knowledgeable.

You should have patience with your wife and help her to achieve righteous objectives with an emphasis on the acquisition of knowledge. Whereas if you are married to sisters who may be beautiful and attractive to you, but have no knowledge of Islam or she is not a Muslim, and later on some disagreement should develop between both of you which becomes problematic, instead of seeking Islamic solutions she will be more inclined to go back to her Jaaliheyya ways of life to look for solutions for that is what she knows and you cannot blame her for that.

You should try to be just and exerciser patience, and depend upon the nature of the problem, weather the fault is yours or not, you should try and explain to her the Islamic solution if one can be found based upon the Book and the Sunnah of the Prophet (pbuh)

Likewise, for sisters who are looking for husbands, I advise you to look for brothers who fear Allah, brothers who have good companions, brothers who are going to circles to gain knowledge of the Deen in all its forms with the correct understanding of the Salaf in order to implement it in their lives, brothers who are described as having Taqwah. (Taqwah see p25).

That is my recommendation to my sisters who are looking for a good husband.

Once again, I am grateful to our brother for sharing some of his married and divorce life's experiences with us; I hope these experiences may be of some benefit to at least some of my readers in protecting their marriage from the quite often pain and regrets associated with divorce.

Case Study 3

Mr. Abdullah

(Q) Brother my first question to you is how and under what circumstances did you meet your wife?

(A) First, I would like to say I have already been happily married when I decided to take a second wife to which my present wife had no objection.

However, to answer your question I was introduced to her by a friend who introduced me to her uncle who was acting as her walli due to the absence of her father who is residing in another country.

(Q) After how many meetings and after what period did you both decided to get married?

(A) We had approximately four meetings and two supervised phone conversations, over a period of four weeks before we mutually agreed to get married.

(Q) Did you also meet her family, and did you find them welcoming and accommodating towards you during those four weeks of meetings and getting to know each other?

(A) Yes, everybody that matters including her father, uncles, and other members of her family were very happy and nice to me excluding her mother.

(Q) What was she unhappy about, and did she object to the marriage and if so, what was her reason or reasons for objecting?

(A) According to what I was made to understand from the rest of her family, she was unhappy with me because I was not of the same race and nationality as she and the rest of her family.

(Q) What race and nationality are they from?

(A) They are from Somalia.

(Q) But Somalis are black people just like you, and although you are from a different country the important fact that binds you and her together is that you are all Muslims, and the greater fact is, Islam does not discriminate against people on the basis of colour, race or nationality.

Therefore, my question is how can this lady's objection be justified?

(Q) Permit me to say that if this lady has truly based her objection to the marriage because of racism, nationalism, tribalism, or any otherism, then this behaviour was addressed by Allah in the Holy Quran some fourteen hundred years plus ago, so I will sight it and leave it for my readers to draw their own conclusion.

وَإِذْ قُلْنَا لِلْمَلَٰٓئِكَةِ ٱسْجُدُوا۟ لِـَٔادَمَ فَسَجَدُوٓا۟ إِلَّآ إِبْلِيسَ أَبَىٰ وَٱسْتَكْبَرَ وَكَانَ مِنَ ٱلْكَٰفِرِينَ

"And when We said unto the angels: Prostrate yourselves before Adam, they fell prostrate, all save Iblis. He demurred through pride, and so became a disbeliever. (2/34.

Therefore, by virtue of this verse of the Quran it is safe to say that any Muslim who discriminates against any human bean because of race or colour is declared a disbeliever by Allah just as He declared Iblis a disbeliever.

(A) Well, that was the conclusion of the rest of the family who did not support the view of the mother, so based upon that conclusion we proceeded with the marriage.

(Q) So eventually you both agree to get married with the consent of the father, the uncle who was the wakeel, and rest of the family?

(A) Yes.

(Q) Did you have an Islamic and secular marriage or only an Islamic marriage?

(A) We had an Islamic marriage in the Masjid.

(Q) Now you are married to her Masha-Allah, how long did it take both of you to come to terms with your differences and begin to settle down peacefully as man and wife?

(A) By the second night.

(Q) To repeat what you said, you say "by the second night" what do you mean by that, can you elaborate?

(A) Well on the second night of the marriage I was at her home and what she did to me I can only described it as one of the saddest day or night of my life. For by her actions regretfully sad thing began to manifest.

(Q) You said sad and regretful things begin to manifest. Would you like to share some of those experiences with us, which made you describe these experiences as sad? What was the problem that you found with her that gave you cause for concern? Was she uncooperative, was there a problem with yourself, what was your experience that made you described it as a sad day, and a sad night?

(A) It was her behaviour

(Q) Did this behaviour last for a short while and then it stopped, or was it continuous and because of this continued behaviour it eventually led to the divorce?

(A) It was continuous.

(Q) Did you seek or have meditation to find solution to the problem?

(A) We did not seek help together, but I sought advice, and I was advised to have patience, but since the problem was based upon trustworthiness and negation of my rights, I had to start thinking about my future.

For example, in the meetings we had before the marriage, I told her I do not want to have any problems with you, and if you know there is going to be problems between us such as arguments, or issues relating to any of your past relationship then don't marry me, and her reply was there will be no problems.

(Q) Let me put this question to you, as you may be aware. In an Islamic marriage, one of the fundamental pillars is based upon rights and obligations and I am taking it for granted that you are aware of them?

(A) Yes, I am aware of them.

(Q) So my next question is related to your rights as a husband, where they respected and upheld by your wife?

(A) No, they were not.

(Q) Also, her rights which are your obligations, is to feed her, cloth her, shelter her, and give her the necessary securities, to name a few. Were you upholding these obligations to her?

(A) Yes, most definitely.

(Q) To be more specific, let us look at some of your rights that she is obligated to uphold. Some of the areas of her obedience to you are, she should obey you in that which is lawful in terms of who she associates with, her going out, protecting yours and her honour and property in your absence, your rights in terms of her fidelity, respond to you sexually if she is well and capable. Were these rights upheld?

(A) I found her very disobedient and unwilling, for a while I was fulfilling her rights, but she would ignore mine. For example, on the second night of our marriage I attempted to hug her but she refused by resisting my advances, and when I asked her what the problem was, she simply said to me divorce me. When I asked her why she wanted this divorce, she refuses to explain or give me any reason for her behaviour or her request for a divorce. Rather her behaviour became very argumentative and incoherent.

Finally, after patiently requesting that if I am to give her the divorce, she is asking for at least I have a right to know the reason. It was at that point she told me that she still had feelings for her ex-husband.

(Q) Now at least you began to understand what the main problem was, how did you deal with it? Did you shout at her calling her bad names, break down and cry, become truly angry, walk away, what did you do?

(A) At that point I was totally gutted hearing such a statement coming from the woman I have just married. If she had told me this during the negotiation before we got married it would have been up to me to choose whether to marry a woman who still had feelings for her ex-husband.

To me it was very unfair and disturbing hearing such statements coming from my wife. Could anyone imagine me saying to my wife on the second day of our marriage "I am missing my other wife and I want to go home". I wonder how any woman whether first or second would feel. Although this could be true to say it to one's wife or husband, it is very disrespectful and unfair.

At that moment a lot of different ideas came to my head, some good, some evil, but eventually I decided to go to the Masjid and all praise are due to Allah Who has guided me to Islam through which I was able to reject the evil thoughts remembering that Allah said "Your wives and your children are a fitnah for you".

Having arrived there, I prayed and asked for guidance and finally I decided to give it another chance thinking maybe she is confused, or she has not got much sense, or she do not know how to express herself in a proper way.

With the best of intentions, I eventually went back to the house and invited her to discuss what had taken place. After a lengthy discussion, she apologised and promised that such a thing will never happen again, and asked me to forgive her, which I did although this experience has left a bitter and hurtful feeling in my heart.

(Q) You said remorsefully she asked you to forgive her, and you did but with some reservations. So, my question is, how was her attitude and behaviour in the days, weeks, or months that followed?

(A) Things carried on reasonably well for a while, and one day I came home and found she had put some henna on her feet which looked exceptionally beautiful, so I took a picture of it with my mobile phone. Later on, I went back to my first wife's home and knowing how inquisitive women I can be erased them just in case my first wife should see it and start asking awkward questions.

Sometime later I returned to my second wife's home and she asked me to show her the pictures of her feet that I have taken, and I told her I had erased them.

She immediately became terribly angry, she started to say you do not love me, you prefer your first wife more than me, it is better you divorce me and go back to your other wife.

At that moment I felt as if I have had enough so I got up, got dressed and told her I am going, I cannot deal with your mood swings anymore, I am leaving.

She immediately got, up came up to me saying I am sorry, I am sorry I didn't mean to hurt you please forgive me, please forgive me, and she kept on pleading, so I sat down and listened to her and at that point I felt sorry for her, so I said ok I forgive you, but this has to stop. Then she said ok but there is something else that I want from you.

What followed was a request from her which if I agree or accept would breach the agreement she wanted when we first met, and negotiations were going on before our marriage. In those negotiations she requested that I should only spend one day per week with her and the rest with my first wife because she had to look after her sister who was terribly ill.

My response was, "are you sure this is what you want? What about your rights of me spending the days that you are entitled to with you?" Her reply was no it's ok that is what I want. So I agreed and until this point in our marriage, I was only spending one night per week with her and I would visit her one day per week.

I then asked her what it is that you want from me. She said I want you to spend more time with me, so I want you to give me all the time I am entitled to, whether it is three or four nights per week.

My immediate response was no, for that was not the agreement you wanted when we first met and based upon the only choice I had to accept, I have certain agreements with my other family which cannot be changed overnight.

Straight away her responses were then divorce me, divorce me, go back to your other wife, you do not love me.

Suggestions

(Q) Let me interrupt you for a moment to address a few points you made or else it may get lost in the chain of your narrations.

Based upon what you have explained regarding the chain of events that took place when she got angry about the missing pictures that you took off her feet being hennaed, and then she demanded that you divorce her, and then she apologised.

Secondly her request for you to spend more time with her by increasing the number of nights you spend with her.

Based upon my understanding and observation regarding the different episode and events that have taken place in the marriage which finally reached to the present situations that you are describing; I have a few comments or suggestions I would like to offer to which you may agree or disagree.

First let me reiterate that it is your right to agree or disagree with whatever I have to say regarding this matter because I am sure you know this lady and I do not, so I must give you that respect.

I believe your experiences and how you dealt with your wife's questions could produce some benefit to our readers who may find themselves in a similar situation; so, if you have no objection let us explore this development between you and your ex-wife to see what lesson or lessons can be taken from your actions and experiences. Could another approach by yourself result in a more positive result than the one you had?

My first point refers to the way in which you dealt with the issue of admitting to your second wife the reasons for erasing from your phone the pictures you took of her hennaed feet. Let us reflect and look at another response that you could have offered.

Do you think if you had simply apologised for erasing the pictures, saying although I liked them, I was not sure whether you liked them being taken? However, since you were pleased with them, I would be happy to take then again.

Do you think this sort of reply would have had a more positive impact on your relationship?

My second point is about her request to have the time you spent with her extended. Looking back at the first two days and nights you spent with her which you described as sad, and the final reason she admitted being the cause for her behaviour, was her still having feelings for her ex-husband'.

When I put all these events into context, problematic and hurtful as they may be, I can see a woman who has had quite a bit of marital problems in the past, and she is not sure who to trust and she is still having doubts about you or men generally. So, she is wondering to herself are you going to be different, and as she is going through a sort of emotional turmoil of uncertainty, she is putting you to the test.

However, I think something you did had caught her attention, and it attracted her emotionally, and she is beginning to see or find something in you that impresses and attracts her. So, the barriers are slowly coming down and she has begun to feel a bit safer, relaxed, and settled, although there is still some doubt in her mind may be because of past behaviour and experiences.

She has now decided to put a pause on her resistance to you and take a chance to prove a point, and to satisfy that desire she has decided to spend some more time with you, her husband.

It is therefore my opinion that her choice of actions are only the building blocks to help to strengthen the weak confidence in herself based upon her fear of being rejected. I think she was finding it difficult to express herself, maybe because of her feeling of guilt of her own negative contribution to the relationship so far.

To be brief, taking her culture and tradition into consideration her actions and recent statements suggest to me that she is saying the trial period of our relationship is almost over, and I would like to make up for lost time and spend some quality time with my new husband, and Allah knows best. So as opposed to the way you handled the discussion with her, I believe if you had simply said to her, 'is that what you really want'?

Then wait for the reply, to which I believe she would have said yes. Now you say to her this would be good/nice, but let me think about it because due to what you wanted previously some changes or new arrangements

would have to be made with the other family in order to accommodate this. Then ask her is that ok; what do you think, or how about that?

(Q) Having heard my points of view, do you think I could be right, or if you did what I am saying or something similar, would it have produced a positive response from her, or it would have been a complete waste of time, so it would not have made any difference to the situation? Like I said before you know this lady and I do not.

(A) Yes, I think you are right. When I reflect and take a closer look at the situations how they gradually develop from a discussion to an argument, to a conflict, I think I made some mistakes in the way I handled that specific situation. In the beginning when I told my first wife, I will only be giving my second wife just one night per week, she disagreed and told me to give her, her full rights. So, I do not think my first wife would have had any problems with me spending some more time with her.

Looking back, when she asked me to spend some more time with her, I should have just agreed and sort it out later with my first wife.

As for the pictures again, yes you could be right, my actions could and should have been different in the way I dealt with the situation, but then it all has to do with experience, and mistakes have been made but we are all imperfect humans on a learning curve.

(Q) So, there you are, although you were right in going back to the contractual agreement of the marriage where she requested that you only spend one night and a day with her and you both agreed to it, that agreement does not necessarily close the door to Rahman (mercy) when it becomes necessary. However, since you have admitted those mistakes have been made and no man is perfect, I ask Allah to forgive you and myself for our mistakes Amen. For Allah is most Forgiving Merciful.

(A) Another problem we had was she requested that whenever I am with her please advise your other wife not to text or call you.

This was agreed and maintained by my first wife, but when I am with my first wife she would be texting and calling me, so what do you think this is doing to my heart? This is telling me that she is not trustworthy neither is she fair.

(Q) Was your first wife aware that she was texting and calling you?

(A) I try and keep it away from her, but I believe she knew but kept quiet about it. When I say to my second wife you are doing exactly what you asked my first wife not to do, she just simply ignores me. So, with all this plus her other behaviour how can I trust her. I told her I want to love you for who you are so please desist from this unnecessary behaviour.

(Q) With all these unfortunate experiences that you had, have there been some good or happy times with her, and if so, can you name some of them?

(A) Yes, the good times I can remember is when I visited her home and the house would be tidy, and perfumed, we would eat together and that would be nice, and sometimes she would comb my beard, and as she knows a lot of Quran, she would sometimes recite some Quran for me to listen to, and I loved and enjoyed that.

(Q) Masha-Allah.

(A) Were there any children produced from the marriage, and if so, how many, and what are their sexes?

(A) Yes, we have one child together which is a girl.

(Q) Masha-Allah.

(Q) How old is the girl?

(A) She is only one and a half week old.

(Q) So, this baby was born after the divorce?

(A) Yes.

(Q) Were you happy to be a father, and are you looking forward to bringing your daughter up with the co-operation of her mother?

(A) Yes, I would love to, I would love to do that, and furthermore I would like us to act according to the Sunnah, that if she should get married to someone else the child would be given to me, but we both should be involved in the bringing up of our daughter.

(Q) My next question is what the relationship between you and her family was e.g., mother, father, brothers and sisters, uncles, aunts, etc. Was it good, reasonable?

Ie, not good, or bad?

(A) As for her mother I did not meet her before the marriage, but I met her recently and she is an elderly person who seems genuinely nice and polite to me.

(Q) Do you think she has now been good and polite because you are now divorced?

(A) From what I have been told she was resentful because I was not from her country, which is Somalia, not from her tribe, and I am from a different race but as time goes by, she would have come around, but from what I know of her now, she is a good woman.

As for the rest of the family, I have met the three uncles they are okay. One of them was the walli to my wife. As for the father I have never met him because he lives in another country, but he gave permission to one of his brothers to be the wakeel to his daughter, so he is alright.

(Q) Now you have reached a point where it has become clearly operant that your marriage to this sister has broken down, and it's not working out, you are both heading for separation.

I would like you to tell us what effort were made by yourself or your wife in seeking advice and help from the families, or from some respectable knowledgeable experience person who deals with the matrimonial problems, to try and bring about a solution to the on-going problems, or a peaceful reconciliation between both of you?

(A) The answer is none, with exception of myself who was advising her to have patience and to fear Allah, and even after the divorce was agreed upon, I offered to fulfil her rights in terms of food, clothes, and shelter, until the baby was born while the divorce was pending, she refused my help so there is nothing I could do.

(Q) Was the final decision to divorce based upon her constant demands from your wife or was it your decision?

(A) Her contribution was also a factor in my decision, but ultimately it was my decision.

(Q) To me there seems to be some inconsistency for rather than a mutual decision between you both to divorce there sensed to be what I could only describe as an unbalanced or one-sided decision here. So, to clarify any doubt that may be assumed, let me put this question to you for since this interview started you have never given us the impression that you really wanted to divorce this lady.

So the question is; am I correct in assuming that irrespective of what had taken place between your wife and yourself if she had not insisted on you divorcing her, you would still have patiently try to preserve the marriage?

(A) Yes, that is correct.

(Q) May Allah reward you for your patience and your intention. However, it seems there was no separation or reconciliation before the divorce?

A) No there was no separation before the divorce; and once the divorce was initiated, I had to move out of her house.

(Q) So you initiated the divorce to her, how many times did you pronounced divorce to her?

(A) Two times

(Q) So, the door of reconciliation is still open through marriage?

(A) Yes.

(Q) If the opportunity should present itself again would you consider remarrying your ex-wife?

(A) No not. You do not get stung by putting your hand in the same hole twice.

(Q) Are there any amicable agreements between you and your ex-wife for the future of your daughter?

Yes, we have a verbal but mutual agreement that I will look after my daughter as long as it is possible.

(Q) Looking back, do you have any regrets regarding the outcome of this episode of your life?

(A) No, no regrets.

(Q) It is obvious that you have accumulated a wealth of experience about married life and unfortunately also divorce, but it is also clear that you are still happily married to your first wife.

Has this recent experience which you have described cause you to change your views about polygamy, so you will now just settle down with as they say the love of your life, or you may sometime in the future take a second wife?

(A) First of all, I think polygamy is an exceptionally beautiful institution which Allah has permitted, so I embrace it wholeheartedly.

From this experience I have learnt quite a few things, such as how to exercise patience, also the knowledge of how to seek a wife by being more thorough when looking into her background and her lineage.

I can also see the benefits of marring someone from your own community instead of going out, for you will have a better knowledge of their history.

You will be more aware of where they are coming from; you will have a more in-depth knowledge of their lineage their culture, and their language. When one is equipped with this knowledge of a sister the likelihood of misunderstandings and problems in a marital relation will be minimized or less likely to happen.

So yes, I would do it again my experience is only a test from Allah in which I have learned more about the principles of justice, of how to be reasonable, and above all to fear Allah in this institution.

Once again may Allah reward you for the contributions you have made to this research, and hopefully it will be of tremendous benefit to mankind generally.

Case Study 4

Mr & Mrs Abd Allah

Since this interview is joint between Mr and Mrs Abd Allah in their answers, I will just abbreviate W for the wife and H for the husband or W&H for affirmations

(Q) So, my first question is how you met your husband and when did you get married.

(A-W) We met when we were at college and we got married one year later in September of two thousand and nine. (H. agrees)

(Q) How long were you married before the problems which led to the divorce began?

(A) The problem was going on for quite a while, but three weeks before the divorce it reached a point of, as they say no return.

(Q) Do you want to talk about the problems?

(A-W) No (H. agrees)

(Q) Did any of you seek the help of mediation before you both agree to divorce each other?

(A-W) No it was my fault it was my entire fault because I should have gone to my dad who is my walli, but I did not want to upset him, because I know he would be very unhappy if he knew his daughter was getting divorce. (H) Anyway, when she did go to him it was too late to do anything about it.

(Q) Do think that was a wise move?

(A-H) No for when she finally did, it was too late for any reconciliation.

(Q) Forgive me but allow me to make a comment, based one of the problems I have found with Muslims today is that they do not recognise or respect the position of the walli after the wedding has taken place. The walli is an especially important pillar in the marriage of any two people and after the marriage he is still there for consultation and mediation in times of problems.

He is your first port of call-in times of uncontrolled behaviour from yourselves. Any way in this book I am writing the Importance of Walliship, has been expounded

(Q) Which of you first came up with the idea and suggested that divorce was the only justified solution to the on-going problem that was prevalent at the time?

A W) It was me; you could say I am a very impatient or I am spoil, for If I say something repeatedly about a situation that needs to be dealt with, and it is not rectified, then I am not going to just sit around doing nothing, and when I look at the things that was going on at that time in our marriage, I believe that my reasons for asking for a kullah was justified.

(Q) I have listened carefully to what you have just said including taking responsibility for your impatience, so to me it seems that you are implying that your husband was either not listening or paying attention to what you were saying regarding the problems that was going on at that time.

(A/W) Yes that is correct for although I admit that I am an impatient person I waited a long time for my husband to do something about the problems I was bringing to his attention, but although we would talk about it no action was taken by him to change the situation, and just as my son if I tell him to behave himself again and again and he do not behave himself then I am going to do something about it

Having said that I did take some time to look at myself with respect to my contribution to the problem, and having done that I realised that I was also blameworthy in as far as my obligations to him as a wife, so based upon that I concluded that we should give the marriage a second chance.

(Q) You have heard what your wife said regarding this affair, so my question to you is do 'you think she is impatient'?

(A /H) Yes sometimes she is impatient.

(Q) Another question to you is 'why did you not pay more attention to the complaints coming from your wife'?

(A) I would say as someone who procrastinates, I am very laid back, and sometimes there are things she would say to me and I would not take any immediate notice of what she would say, however after sometime I would reflect on what she has said and would act on it but by then it was too late.

Now looking back, type equation here. I think that was one of the main the cause of the downfall of the relation.

Comment (2)

(Q) Sometimes we think it may be ok to be laid back, but when your wife is calling your attention to an issue that is having a negative impact on the marriage do you think it is wise or is there any benefit to assume this position of being laid back. Rather do not think that you should listen attentively and take these matters seriously enough to do something about it.?

(A) Yes, I agree.

(Q) Are there any children from the marriage, and if so, how many and what are their age?

(A H) One son and he is three years old.

(Q) During the separation were you missing your son, and were you both missing each other?

(A /H/W) Very much I missed my son and I missed my wife, and the same applied to me although I had our son living with me, I missed my husband this is a person that I have live with for some three years and the next thing you know he is gone, I had no adult companion in the home that I had become accustomed to, this is a strange feeling of belonging, so yeah, I missed my husband.

(Q) Which of you first came up with the idea that divorce was the only solution left to bring the on-going problem to an end?

(A /H) It was my wife; I think she came to a point where she though enough is enough and she asked me for a divorce and I just agreed to it.

(Q) The reason your wife gave you for the divorce was it a valid one or you gust you just agree to it because she asked you?

(A/H) That was not the first time she asked me for a divorce and previously I disagreed but, on this occasion, I agreed because whatever was going on was to her dissatisfaction, and she said it was enough.

(Q) Was it Talaq or Kullah?

(A/H) It was kullah.

(Q) Why Kullah.

(A/W) Because previously when I asked him for a divorce, he refused so this time I insisted on a separation and I asked for a kullah, so I gave him back the mahr and he agreed to accept the kullah.

(Q) How long after the separation you began to think about what has really happened?

(A/H) It was less than three weeks.

(W) It was less than three weeks, but from the very next day after the divorce I began to think about what my life is going to be from now on without my husband and is this what I really want for myself and my son, without his father around to help to bring him up.

(Q) Are you saying that your experience after a day of being divorced brought you to the conclusion that the advantage of married life outweighs the disadvantage of separation?

(A/W) Yes, the advantage of being together far outweighs the disadvantage of separation yes that is correct.

(Q) Was this a mutual feeling of both of you as described by your wife?

(A/H) I could have gone off and married another woman, she could have found another husband, but the fact is there are times as they say some things are there worth fighting for, plus I know it is difficult for a young woman to raise a child on her own in this sort of society.

Also, when I think of my son been brought up without his father being around, helps me to make the decision of reconciliation much easier.

(Q) How did you both went about seeking reconciliation, was it through a third party or one of you made the first approach?

(A/H) I went to my mother and she made the approach to her and then we went to see her father.

(Q) Your husband made the first attempt towards reconciliation, was this something that you were pleased with and gave you the encouragement to act positively?

(A/W) Yes, for I knew from the onset if it was up to my husband we would be divorced, but when you are angry and someone is apologising to you it will take you sometime to calm down and accept their apology. So although it wasn't too hard for me to accept it did take some time for me to calm down and see and accept the benefits of reconciliation.

(Q) Looking back at this episode of your lives including the fact that as you have stated it was you the wife who demanded and implemented the divorce and now you are both happily remarried.

What lesson or lessons have you learned from this experience, giving the chance to relive your life again, share with us some of the lessons and benefits you have both learnt from these experiences?

(A/W) Yes, I have learnt some lessons. As for me being a Muslima the way I behaved in some cases could have been better, but the way I reacted to some of the things that was going on, I have no apology for my behaviour in those contexts, however as I say the way I behaved in some cases being a Muslim woman I do have some regrets.

Observation

(Q) Will you allow me to put forward an observation based upon what you have stated so far?

(A) OK

You have made some particularly important decisions regarding the direction you took that finally led up to the divorce between you and your husband. It is therefore obviously clear to those who understand the Islamic criteria in dealing with matters of divorce that you have ignored some of the correct protocols in dealing with such matters weather out of ignorance or deliberate, and here I am not judgemental upon you I am just stating the facts.

However, the facts speak for themselves, for Allah has put into place the correct checks and balances in dealing with matters of this nature. For example, there was no arbitration, or consultation with your walli who is also your father until after the divorce. This is not correct from an Islamic point of view, seeing that you both did not take the necessary steps that may have saved the marriage before it reached the point of no return.

So here the importance of the walli cannot be over emphasised for marriage brings two families together and one of the attributes of learning is to do things in a better way. So as young Muslims we should take some time out to study the Fiqh of marriage, for the walli being one of its fundamental pillars should be recognised in terms of his importance.

Therefore, going forward it could be beneficial if you both sit with your dad/walli and discuss his role in your marriage from an Islam point of view.

(Q) Looking back at whatever led both of you to decide that divorce was the only option left for you to settle your difficulties, do you think that anger played a major part in coming to the decision to divorce?

(A/W) Yes anger played a major part in it for it was more me than my husband who demands divorce when I got angry and demanded a kullah. (Q) Now based upon a mutual agreement between yourselves you have agreed to be remarried. Masha-Allah you have done so. Now my question has two parts. The first part is 'what lessons have one or both of you learn from the experience of separation, and the benefits of renewing your marital commitments'?

(A/W) One of the lessons I have learnt is based upon giving my husband more quality time, I am at university, and he is busy working, so we do not have a lot of time for each other, and on top of all that we have a young son to look after. I do not think I gave my husband sufficient time in the past for we are both busy and sometimes I am tired, but now that has changed, and I can see the benefits and the reward coming back to me by fulfilling his rights.

As for being remarried I am incredibly happy to be remarried to my husband rather than to be married to someone else that I am not accustomed to being with. As for my experience of being divorced is this something I would like to go through again. The answer is no way.

So, the lessons learnt is the disadvantage of being alone with my son without his father, and the benefits of being with my husband and the father of my son, so I am very, very happy that I have remarried my exhusband, and our son is very happy to have dad at home again.

(A/H) One of the most important lessons I have learnt from this experience is how important my wife was, and is, to me. I now realise that in the past I took a lot for granted as a husband.

In the past I would have expected her to wash, to cook and clean look after the baby without realising that she can be as tired as I am. Now this is something of the past and now we help each other. I am also glad that we are remarried for I have learnt from the mistakes of the past.

(A/W) One of the lessons I have learned as a wife, and I would like to give as an advice to my sisters and anyone going through marital problems and is thinking about divorce, is to remember the day you got marry and reflect on the happiness you felt. Then think about the things you did that brought about that situation and feeling of joy and tranquillity. So, the advice is simply to go back to that experience.

The stress and strains of life sometimes cause you to forget who you are and what your functions as a wife/husband are supposed to be. For example, taking home too much homework can also play a major role in destabilising a family, so we have to be just in giving each responsibilities its due right; for being up until two in the morning trying to complete an assignment, and getting very little sleep makes one grumpy, so we should learn to measure correctly the length of time we spend on each task.

(A/H) My contribution to the subject based upon my experience is that we should never underestimate the value of patience. Patience will get you over many hurdles. Many of the problems I had with being married was only a test from Allah and if I had used the experience for the benefit of my family maybe there would never have been any divorce.

So my advice to my brothers out there is to have patience and transparency with their wives and communicate with each other and let she know how you feel. Once again Jazaakum Allahu Khiran to both of you and all those who have contributed to this research for your contributions to this narrative, hopefully it may have a positive effect on those unfortunate couples who are facing or contemplating divorce, or whom my unfortunately find themselves in a similar situation as you have all been through.

Advice to the Muslims in the West

By virtue of the research, I have conducted in developing this book, it has given me an accurate and factual account of each paragraph that I have presented.

So, since each of the issues presented here are based upon facts and substantiated evidence and experience, I will attempt to offer some sincere advice to my brothers and sisters.

However, before I attempt to offer some advice let me make a brief comment on the last case study we have been privileged to share with this couple, may Allah preserve them.

Through my experience I also bear witness to cases that is very prevalent among married couple whose wife has decided to take up a degree course in any subject of their choice to gain a profession.

There is nothing wrong with our wives being intelligent, but even with the best of medication that cures an illness, it sometimes produces a side effect that is difficult to cure.

And if the student of knowledge is aware of the side effects of being a student which consumes a lot of time and sacrifice which often impacts upon family relation, be it the husband, the children and other than them, and if they are not prepared to deal with it rationally, intelligently and patiently, it can sometimes result in the destruction of marital and family relation.

For as we all know, being a wife and the mother to the family is more than a full-time job, having to wash, cook, clean, looking after the children, taking them to school and collecting them, doing the shopping sometimes, plus fulfilling her obligations as a wife to her husband to name but a few, is not an easy task unless she has an understanding helpful husband.

Now to be taking on studying for degree with all that it entails of reading and researching, studying and writing to complete assignments on time staying up late at nights, and a lot of loss of sleep and well-deserved rest, will take up a large portion of her time that she would normally have spent fulfilling her obligation of being a wife, a mother, and a housewife, this can, and will put a large strain on the family relationship.

Therefore, when this is not understood by both parties in the relationship, husband and the wife, and handled properly, it will only lead to stress, arguments, anger, and in some cases nervous breakdown, which is a recipe for divorce.

So, for this change of lifestyle to be trouble free it will nictitate a patient, helpful, and understanding husband who is prepared to fill in the blank spaces that the wife will not be able to full for a while, and also be prepare to give up some of his expected quality time.

If this is understood, and all these checks and balances are put into place, regarding the wife maintaining the proper adabh and aqlak in the college or university environment where free mixing is the norm, then I say to my brother husbands help your wives to get her degree for there are benefits in it since an intelligent wife will help to produce intelligent off springs.

That been Said among the people whom I have spent quite a bit of time with are Arabs, Asians, and Africans, and they have preceded most of us in the religion of Islam. 'Us' meaning those of us who were born and brought up in the west, and in a religion other than Islam.

I will now attempt to share one of the many beneficial lessons than I have learnt while living with and learning from these people.

One of the most important aspects of their lives that held my attention and interest was that although they were all belonging to the same one nation, they were divided into different tribes and in most case, they share a national language, traditions, customs and culture, religion, eating habits, sports and governance.

However, each tribe would have their own specific dialectal language, custom, culture, food, and tradition still, these differences neither oppose nor interfere with the good relationship between the different tribes. In terms of marital relations in some cases, marriage only takes place within their own specific tribe, or family, while in some cases they would be allowed to marry outside their own tribe but only to their own national.

As for those of us in the West, this would be portrayed as being racist (assabeya), but for the people who have these traditions for hundreds of years as a major aspect of their cultures and their way of life, it offers them great benefit and guarantees peace and security within the nation and the extended family.

As we know in Islam it is accepted, and it is also of great benefit to be married to someone who is not only known to the bride and groom but is also known to the families of each partner. For when the history of the people is common knowledge between the families, the questions regarding linage, wealth, piety, customs, and culture which are paramount to making constructive decisions to allow a marriage is enhanced.

Based upon such knowledge gained through my association with these different nations and tribes, I came to realise how easy it has been for them, and continue to be, in settling disputes between husbands and wives before it reaches the point of no return.

So, the rate of divorce among these nations are far less than those of us who live in this diverse, multi-racial, multi-cultural, multi religious, multi-ethnic society.

So, we can see in these marriages which has its roots in a racial, tribal, cultural custom, with the proper Islamic guidelines, the relationship between the wife and the husband has to be much more secured than the marriage that came about as a result of two strangers from two different nationalities, different cultures and customs deciding to get married after a few briefs arranged meetings in a mosque or any other arranged meeting place.

On the other hand, marriages that are based upon what is described as brief meetings by two people who hardly know each in the above paragraph contain a greater risk of been problematic than the those that has its roots in nationality, culture and tribal customs.

This does not mean that I am suggesting that we cannot have a happy and durable marriage outside our own nationality, culture and custom, but the foundation of the marriage must be based upon piety, and these differences are known, understood and accepted by both partners. When this is known and properly understood, these differences can bring happiness, cultural benefits, diversity, and education to the marriage that helps to prolong a long and happy married life.

I hope these examples I am sighting may help us to understand why although we are all Muslims, and we have learnt that discrimination among Muslims must be based only on Taqwah. How often men who chose to marry sisters from a different race, are faced with objections from the families of Muslim sisters who chose to marry outside their own nationality.

So before we become judgemental upon these people we must first begin to understand where they are coming from in terms of their culture, and their traditions, for although they have left their native land for whatever reason, it does not mean that they have left their traditions and their culture behind weather it is religious or secular, rather it is a part of their innate way of life just like the kind of food they have always eaten, and the type of clothe they have worn for centuries from one generations to another.

They are not going to give up their traditional food for fish and chips just because they are now living in Great Britain, rather they set up their own restaurant and produce their own traditional dishes knowing that it will be bought and eaten by their own people and other than them. This has in some way benefitted them for centuries and it will not disappear overnight just because they have migrated to a different country. Also, they will manufacture them clothe to suit another tradition and culture irrespective of the weather.

It must be understood that these traditions and culture is the way of life for millions of people from different parts of the world. So, what we must do is to weigh up these practices on the scale of haram and the halal to see if what they have been and continue to be upon is allowed. If they are in line with the Book and the Sunnah, we say Jazzah kum Allahu Khiran, but if it is not, we say Fear Allah through whom we claim our rights.

Biddah is one of the most destructive actions that any Muslim can embark upon, for although it is wrong to the extent that it becomes a lie against Allah and His Prophet (pbuh) and a guarantee for the one who is upon it to enter the hell fire, the irony is that many of those who are upon Biddah do not see it as going astray from the right path even when the proofs and evidence are presented to them.

As a matter of fact, they see it as something commanded in the Shariah so they will never repent and turn away from it. So, for us to be fair we must look at the history of these people and see where they are today based upon their way of life, and if the advantage of these practices outweighs the disadvantages then we say carry on as usual, but if it does not, we present them with the proofs, and invite them to return to the Book and the Sunnah, and the Faham of the Salaf.

Sometimes Allah allows a people to behave badly for a time, it is called respite. He did with many of the people of the past, then He the Merciful send signs and warmers to them that they may take heed of their ways and implement the necessary changes to their lives that will not only benefit them but will be pleasing to Allah.

However, when they reject the advice and the call for change, He sometimes displace and destroy them and leave their history as a witness, a sign and an evidence for those who understand. So, I say to those who find themselves in this ill-begotten situation, think deeply and consider the statement of Allah which says, "Allah will never change the condition of a folk until they change that which is in their hearts."

So, it is up to us to be judgemental upon ourselves and admit we have done wrong, gone astray, and change the direction that we have been travelling on and return to the book and the Sunnah with the Faham of the Salaf and not the Faham of our forefathers who had no knowledge

لَهُۥ مُعَقِّبَٰتٌ مِّنۢ بَيْنِ يَدَيْهِ وَمِنْ خَلْفِهِۦ يَحْفَظُونَهُۥ مِنْ أَمْرِ ٱللَّهِ ۗ إِنَّ ٱللَّهَ لَا يُغَيِّرُ مَا بِقَوْمٍ حَتَّىٰ يُغَيِّرُوا۟ مَا بِأَنفُسِهِمْ ۗ وَإِذَآ أَرَادَ ٱللَّهُ بِقَوْمٍ سُوٓءًا فَلَا مَرَدَّ لَهُۥ ۚ وَمَا لَهُم مِّن دُونِهِۦ مِن وَالٍ

For him (each person) there are angels ranged before him and behind him, who guard him by Allah's command. (Lo! Allah do not change the condition of a folk until they (first) change that which is in their hearts;) and if Allah will et misfortune for a folk there is none that can repel it, nor have they a defender beside Him. (HQ 13v 11)

As for the new Muslims who may meet in the Masjid attending some classes, conference, lecture, or for the Friday or Eid prayer, a Walima etc. the truth is, we meet as strangers and we depart as strangers, see you next time round. As salamu alaykum. This is the reality of our situation today.

In order to go forward and to address our present situation, we will have to go backward. To where? To Al-Madinah over fourteen hundred plus years ago for it is only in Al-Madinah, the land of the great Hijrah where we will find the models that were left by the Holy Prophet (pbuh) and His Companions (rh) that is going to rectify and address the present stated of the Ummah, and to this effect Allah has informed us in Surah to Al Ahzab.

لَقَدْ كَانَ لَكُمْ فِى رَسُولِ ٱللَّهِ أُسْوَةٌ حَسَنَةٌ لِّمَن كَانَ يَرْجُواْ ٱللَّهَ وَٱلْيَوْمَ ٱلْآخِرَ وَذَكَرَ ٱللَّهَ كَثِيرًا

Indeed in the Messenger of Allah (Muhammad (peace be upon him)) you have a good example to follow for him who hopes for (the Meeting with) Allah and the Last Day, and remembers Allah much. (33v21)

As for us in the West, most of the times we do not even know the name of our next-door neighbour having lived beside them for most of our life's. So, we never experience what I would describe as the ideal society/community and the extended family where everybody knows everybody in the village, and there are no strangers among them.

So, if it is the wife to be, what is her lineage, is she coming from a wealthy family who had their own servants and is respected, is she is well behaved, but you may expect her to clean, cook, and wash your clothed, when she may never have done these things throughout her adult life. Is she a pious sister, since a pious wife will help her husband to get to Jannah or is, she just a pretty faces whose appearance attracts your attention.?

If it is the husband to be, is he a brother who has Taqwah, and is he able to support and take care of you independently, and what is his lineage?

These are not the general rules of engagement for most of us who are living in the west, so just because one of our friend's husband or wife suggested that a brother or a sister is looking for a wife or husband, we begin to think that this is our dreams come true, so we rush head first and emotionally into a marital relationship without following the proper protocols of investigating the nature and character of this person who we are about to entrust our life and future to.

Therefore because of this neglect within a very short space of time things begin to go terrible wrong in the Marriage and as they say, the marriage is on the Rocks, and it is at that point and time we wake up from this emotional matrimonial hurricane, only to realise that this is the worst nightmare I ever had, but it is not a dream, it's a reality for it is happening, and you can turn the back the clock, but you cannot turn back the time, and this is what we are seeing and hearing every day.

So, what should we be doing? We should begin to take more seriously the pillars that Allah has installed in the processes of getting married, also the advice of our beloved Prophet (pbuh) because if any of these pillars are ignored out of ignorance or deliberately, the marriage will be a great fitnah for you, and in some cases invalid. So, let us follow the golden rule, which is in every act of worship, knowledge (MUST) precedes the action, and marriage is one of the greatest acts of worship. As the Prophet (pbuh) said; Marriage completes half the Deen, spend the other half worshiping Allah.

One of fundamental pillars or marriage is Walliship. However, unfortunately many brothers and sisters have taken this particularly important aspect of marriage so lightly, that in some cases it is completely ignored.

In some cases, they think their mother, or a sister can be their Walli, because they have not taken the time out to acquaint themselves with the fundamental pillars of marriage, without which the marriage will be invalid.

Walliship so happens to be one of the pillars in marriage, and although this has been briefly explained on page twelve of this book, I am going to spend a bit more time explaining its importance and the purpose of the Walli in an Islamic marriage.

First, the walli is a man, and not a woman, and if he were not vitally and important in the marriage arrangement, Allah would not have made it (Wajib) compulsory.

Therefore, stressing the importance of the Walli must be understood that he is as important in the marriage as ablution is to the salat, for without ablution, there is no salat, and without the involvement of the Walli in the marriage arrangement there is no marriage.

Since a woman cannot give herself in marriage, it is logical that she must be given by someone and that someone is called the Walli.

There is a false misconception that a woman can be given in marriage to her prospective husband, her mother, or her aunt, her sister, or any female relative. If this ever happens the marriage would be invalid, for the legislation set by Allah and his Rasool is clear. So, who is this Walli?

The Walli of any woman is her father and since in marriage, the father relinquishes his responsibility of Walliship to his daughter's husband, so it becomes the duty and the right of the father to give his daughter in marriage to the man she is going to be married. When this is done, the father surrenders his responsibility as her Walli to his daughter's husband who now becomes her Walli.

However, if this lady accepts Islam and her father has not, the father automatically loses the right to be her Walli.

So, if the father of the girl is not qualified to be her walli then her Muslim uncle, or brother, or her son if she was previously married and has a Muslim son who has reached puberty or the nearest Muslim male relative in her family may assume that responsibility.

As for the revertees who may not have a male Muslim father or relative, then the Imam or a righteous elder, or the Shaykh should be appointed for her as a wakeel, and through him proper protocols are followed to investigate and ascertain all the relevant information that will ensure making the correct decision whether or not she should proceed with the marriage, and if the marriage takes place this walli will be the person to give her in marriage to her new husband. And Allah knows best.

Therefore, speaking as a Muslim, it must be understood that contrary to the false claims and propaganda of the and the misled, our women are regarded to us as the jewels in our crown, and she must be cared for and protected.

Therefore, handing her care and responsibility over to another person is something that must be considered carefully, and Allah has put all the necessary checks and balances in place to ensure that this is done correctly.

So, if any of these fundamental principles are neglected in the marriage, the legality and honour of the relationship between the husband and the wife becomes invalid.

That is as far as the Walli is concerned, and then there has to be two male witnesses, the mahr or gift which the husband is required to gives to the bride.

This can be paid before the wedding, during the wedding, or after the wedding.

Furthermore, this mahr or gift is not a bride price as is portrayed by the misled and the misguided. Another misconception that is practiced in many cultures is where the husband to has got to purchase expensive gifts for the parents and relatives of his intended wife, plus the gift for his intended wife.

There also the cases where it's the wife who has got to pay the mahr to the husband.

It has to be understood that in marriage a man is not purchasing a woman slave, he is seeking a partner with whom he hopes to develop a long and lasting relationship based upon rights and obligations, must, love, respect, care, happiness, companionship, shared responsibilities, families, accountability and responsibility to name a few.

Neither is the mahr to be paid by the bride to the family of bridegroom as is also practiced by some misguided exploiters.

This gift is a token of responsibility that the husband is about to assumes an obligation to care for his wife, and from there onward whatever property or valuables that the wife enters a marriage relationship with is exclusively hers, and whatever her husband has is belonging to him and his wife.

However, if it is agreed to be paid after the wedding, this debt must be honoured and paid by the husband, and he has no right to ask his wife to cancel or forget it, but if she out of her own kindness and generosity offers to cancel this debt, the husband should accept it with gratitude, and that is the only way he can be freed from the obligation of paying her.

Also, unlike the misguided Sect among Muslims, the ceremony must be performed by an Imam and not by the husband.

So let us look at some of the fundamental pillars that should be in place in order to make any Muslim marriage valid according to the Islamic legislation.

They are as follows:

    A. The Walli.

    B. The consent of the woman

Sheikh Mohammad Kamaludin

1. (C) The mahr.
C. Two witnesses.
D. The Imam.

Also, the marriage should not be a secret, but it should be announced or made public to avoid any suspicions of an elicit relationship.

As for changing the customs and attitudes of our brothers and sisters who are in a state of national, tribal, and traditional stupor concerning marital relationship, we must exercise patience and use the proper dowah and example to educate them, and gradually as the younger generations succeed the older ones the changes that reflect the proper Islamic criterion will begin to appear in sha Allah, and Allah knows best.

Another particularly important aspect of marriage is the issue of consent and co-operation of the families of both the prospective husband and that of the wife. The importance of this co-operation cannot be overstated. Therefore, it should be vigorously pursued to ensure their consent and approval, for marriage does not only bring the wife and her husband together, but it also brings two families together.

Finally, although this section of the book is based upon divorce, I have chosen to close it off with an advice to everyone who is in a marital relationship, since marriage is one of the positive sides of human relationship, as opposed to the negative and destructive contribution that divorce has to offer.

Permit me also to explain how the miss used of one of Allah's given attribute and a blessing to human race can become not only an illness but one of the most audient contributor to divorce, and a multitude of other unwelcome problems including death and destruction to name a few.

It is said that to know the cause of a problem is half the cure, and since this destructive illness that I am talking about is the miss use of Anger I would like to offer the treatment to this ever-growing illness which has proven very successful and beneficial to those unfortunates suffers of this illness and Allah help is sought.

Let me also take this opportunity to thank all the contributors to this research

Cultural Perception of Marriage among Muslims

for sharing their marriage and divorce experiences with us, hoping that it may be of some benefit to all those that first who are privileged enough to read this book.

I will now close this section of the book with an advice to all married couple which is;

Hold on to your marriage by all lawful means, and always keep the doors of love and mercy open, and in times of problems, as one of our sisters have advised us 'remember the good times, especially that first week of the marriage' and resort to patience and good advice, and it will close the doors to separation and divorce.

Warning against Anger

I think it is prudent that I should include this subject as an advice not just to all husbands and wives but to mankind in general because of its destructive potentials towards the good relationship between us, human, and of course its destructive effect on a durable and peaceful marriage.

Anger is one of the most ardent tools that the Shaytaan uses to destroy the good relationship between the husband and his wife. Therefore, with the knowledge that to every illness there is a cure, let us try and explore these two opposites: 'Anger and Patience'.

I am also aware that there are individuals who have resorted to unIslamic cultural solutions to address marital problems whenever they may arrive, but I would like to remind my readers that marriage is an institution that Allah Himself has initiated, and the best of husbands were the Prophets, and in this period the best husband is the Prophet Mohammed (pbuh) and since his coming has abrogated all the previous Prophets' legislation the best solution to any problem be it marriage or other than that, must be derived from the Quran and the Sunnah of our beloved Prophet Mohammed (pbuh).

The Purification of the Heart from Anger without Grounds

So, the question is asked. 'What is anger, its nature, and Its potential?

Anger is one of the attributes that Allah has given to humanity which can be used in a positive or a negative way. When it is acted upon or use in the negative way it can be destructive which make the result blameworthy. However, it can also be used positively which is praiseworthy, but that is only when it is kept under control and used to oppose something that is evil, and that is the best course.

The rage of Jaaliheyya or the rage that is based upon the period of ignorance when man had no guidance, was from anger without grounds, without justifiable reason; or cause, hence, it became a curse. Therefore, whosoever uses anger unjustifiably becomes blameworthy. On the other hand, the opposite of anger is described beautifully in the following words patience, forbearance, and perseverance, and Allah praised the believers for their patience, and He bestowed some of the tranquillity on them.

An example of Allah's mercy upon the believer was during the Hijrah of the Prophet (pbuh) from Mecca to Madinah in the company of Abu Bakr (rh). They were pursued by the Mushrikeens of Mecca, so they hid in the Cave, on mount Tho. Observe therefore the Quranic injunction of this incident and how Allah dealt with the people of patience.

إِلَّا تَنصُرُوهُ فَقَدْ نَصَرَهُ ٱللَّهُ إِذْ أَخْرَجَهُ ٱلَّذِينَ كَفَرُوا۟ ثَانِىَ ٱثْنَيْنِ إِذْ هُمَا فِى ٱلْغَارِ إِذْ يَقُولُ لِصَٰحِبِهِۦ لَا تَحْزَنْ إِنَّ ٱللَّهَ مَعَنَا ۖ فَأَنزَلَ ٱللَّهُ سَكِينَتَهُۥ عَلَيْهِ وَأَيَّدَهُۥ بِجُنُودٍ لَّمْ تَرَوْهَا وَجَعَلَ كَلِمَةَ ٱلَّذِينَ كَفَرُوا۟ ٱلسُّفْلَىٰ ۗ وَكَلِمَةُ ٱللَّهِ هِىَ ٱلْعُلْيَا ۗ وَٱللَّهُ عَزِيزٌ حَكِيمٌ

If ye help not (your Prophet), (it is no matter): for Allah did indeed help him, when the Unbelievers drove him out: he had no more than one companion; the two were in the cave, and he said to his companion:

Have no fear, for Allah is with us": then Allah sent down His peace upon him, and strengthened him with forces which ye saw not, and humbled to the depths the word of the Unbelievers. But the word Allah is exalted to the heights: for Allah is exalted in might, Wise. (9/40)

This summary identifies the people who restrain themselves, by protecting their tongue, limbs, and heart from evil, while enjoining the good, forbidding the evil and fearing Allah and the last day.

Therefore, different names may be applied in different situations to the application of enjoining good, while remaining conscious of the opposite, for this is the playing field of Iblis, and we seek refuge in Allah from him and his host. Therefore, enjoining good cannot be achieved unless it is linked to the practice of patience.

So, this shows that Islam in its totality is based on patience as is exemplified in the character of the Prophet of Islam (pbuh) who called his people to Islam for thirteen years and although they abused him, cursed, fought and humiliated him, he exercised supreme patient and did not retaliate physically, and in the end, he was victorious and his message has continued to be victorious until today, and will continue till the end of time.

There were times when he became angry at the people who abused and physically assaulted him due to their opposition of the message he was proclaiming, and the expression of anger could be seen on his face, and his companions would attempt to retaliate, but he would caution them, and advised them to have patient with the people, and point out to his enemies the error of their ways.

Therefore, the lessons to be learn from these beautiful examples of the Prophet (pbuh) is if a person does not possess these beautiful qualities of patience, forbearance, and perseverance, he should realize his own deficiency and then start acting as if he possessed them whenever he or she has been tested, and eventually it will become second nature.

This is the cure, as Allah have stated in His Book.

(Wata waa saw bill haqq, wata waa-saw bi-sabr).

Recommend one another to patience for the (suffering, harm, and injuries one may encounter) while enjoining the good and forbidding the evil HQ. 103.

Let me now draw your attention to the five-letter word Anger, which is one of the human attributes given to us by Allah which can be used praiseworthily, however the misuse of this attribute can become one the of most destructive qualities to be possessed by any human bean. So, let us look at its signs, its classification, and its effects.

The Signs and classification of Anger

The reality of anger is the boiling of the blood of the heart to seek revenge. If a person is angry with someone below them, the blood expands and rises to the face and makes it red. If the person is angry with someone above them, the blood contracts from their outer skin to their heart, and therefore they become sorrowful.

They may begin to cry, develop spasms, and become breathless, talkative, resentful, and abusive. For this reason, they become pale. If they are uncertain as to the status of the person that they are in conflict with, the blood is between contraction and expansion; nevertheless, the person is in a state of rage (semi-lunacy).

3. Degrees of Anger

There are three degrees of anger namely.

1. Insufficient (Tafreet)
2. Excessive (Efrat)
3. Moderate (Ihtidaal)

Tafreet is insufficient anger. It is blameworthy because the one in this state is not angry enough to protest or offer admonition regarding something that is haram (something forbidden). For example, a husband in respect to his family, his wife, daughter or women under his charge, if he has no jealousy at all regarding their conduct, or behaviour, they could conduct themselves in un-Islamic way and he would not be concerned in the least.

They could be walking on the street improperly dressed, without hijab or Jilbab, showing off their awaa, gossiping and associating with other men, and he would not be concerned about their behaviour as female believers, or the responsibility given to him by Allah as a walli. So, he does not exercise his attribute of jealousy and becomes angry for the sake of Allah. So rather than being a servant of Allah entrusted with what Allah has made sacred, he becomes a Dayooth (a wittol), a pimp.

Therefore, o believing men, be careful to your duty to Allah for the Messenger of Allah (pbuh) says in an authentic Hadith one of the people who will not taste the scent of paradise is a Dayooth. Jealousy was created by Allah and placed in the heart of man and woman as a protection when used correctly, but in order not to be blameworthy it must be used in the right context.

Part of this failing is to be silent when you see some objectionable actions, and to be incapable of self-discipline, as since self-discipline is made effective by bringing anger to bear on the appetite.

To be able to say to your internal self, "No, I am a Muslim who Allah has given this responsibility of enjoining good and forbidding evil, therefore how could I even allow myself to think of whatever the Shaytaan suggests, or remain silent after having witnessed that which Allah has made unlawful, except by if doing something to change or stop that evil would have bring about a worst evil than the one I am trying to stop.

Those who believe in Allah and the last day has got an obligation to be angry with themselves if they discover that they are inclines to base appetites of lust and desires. Lack of anger in this context becomes a blameworthy attribute.

If rat is excessive anger, and it is a blameworthy attribute to the possessor. It is to be overcome by anger so that coolness of patience - goes out of the management of the intellect and the deen, and you no longer have insight, time, or patience to investigate the cause of the problem and the effect of retaliation.

Whenever this becomes the case, the three attributes of ifrat falls into place, which are total loss of consideration, reflection, and choice, so the possessor becomes a blind follower of the Shaytaan.

Whenever the fire of anger is intense, it induces mental and spiritual blindness, to the one who is angry, and it will make him or her deaf to every warning, and advice.

As for the Muslim who allows him or herself to be so seduced by Shaytaan, ihsan and taqwah will disappear along with the eemaan. It may increase until anger invades the roots of the senses to the extent that you cannot even see with your eye.

The entire world may become dark, and then eventually it may become so intense that it burns up the moisture which gives life to the heart. The angry person then dies of rage. This is all because they have neglected the golden rules of the Prophetic Sunnah, and the advice of the people of knowledge which gives life which are:

Bring Allah to memory; seek refuge in Allah from the accursed Shaytaan, say Sub Hannah Allah, Al Hamdo li la, wa Laa ill la Laa hu, wa Allahu Akbar. If you are standing, sit down, take deep breath. If you were sitting, lie down; make ablution, and finally, ghusl. Stop, walk away, and say Allahuma sali ala Muhammed, wa ala aalii Muhammed, kama salat ala Ibrahim (etc.).

Say La ilaha ila Allahu al-Azeem al Halim, la ilaha ilaAllah rabbularshi al-Azeem, la illa ha illa Allah rabbus-samawati wa rabbul ardi wa rabbul arshi al karim. (There is no god but Allah, the Great, and the Most Forbearing. There is no god but Allah, the Lord of the Supreme Throne. There is not god but Allah, the Lord of the Heavens, the Lord of the Earth and the Lord of the Great Throne (Bukhari 7/151 and Muslim 4/2092)

ا يَـٰٓأَيُّهَا ٱلَّذِينَ ءَامَنُوٓاْ ٱسْتَجِيبُواْ لِلَّهِ وَلِلرَّسُولِ إِذَا دَعَاكُمْ لِمَا يُحْيِيكُمْ ۖ وَٱعْلَمُوٓاْ أَنَّ ٱللَّهَ يَحُولُ بَيْنَ ٱلْمَرْءِ وَقَلْبِهِۦ وَأَنَّهُۥٓ إِلَيْهِ تُحْشَرُونَ

Oh ye who believe! give your response to God and His Apostle, when He called you to that which will give your life; and know that Allah cometh in between a man and his heart, and that it is He to Whom ye shall (all) be gathered. (8/24)

Consideration, Reflection, Choice.

If this is your situation when you have applied all the above-mentioned solution to yourself and you still cannot control your anger then rest ashore that you do have an anger problem, therefore it is now time for you to see a Muslim counsellor and talk about your problems.

Now ask yourself this question (why do I get angry?)

4. Signs of Ifrat

Among the outward effects of excessive anger are change of colour, extreme intense shaking, and confused speech, foam appearing at the corners of the mouth, redness, and ugly mien. These are the ugly effects of anger on the body.

As far as its effects on the tongue are concerned, it is that you speak with insulting language, obscenity, and ugly words which rational people are ashamed to use. "You talking to me?! Just forget it, I hate you! Go away! I do not care. Leave me alone, I do not want to talk about it. You do not understand, stupid! You make me sick! Shut up! You are always digging me! You dog me! You make me mad! I'll kill you!" And anyone who utters these words is often ashamed of them after their anger has been abated. These are the effects of excessive anger on the tongue.

5. Effects on the Limbs

Is that you strike, tear, wound, and kill, if you are able to do so, without any consideration. If the object of your anger flies, escape, or run away from you, your own anger turns against you yourself, so you begin to cry, tear your own garments and slap your own face, thump some object, break something. You may hit your hand on the ground and completely go beyond the bounds of a chronic drunkard.

You may fall quickly and not be able to stand up through the intensity of your anger. It may come upon you like a fainting spell. You may even hit animals and smash a bowl to the ground, and act like a mad person. You verbally abuse animals and speak to it, saying, "How long can I endure this from you?" As if you were addressing a rational being. These are some of the effects of excessive anger on the heart.

Here Allah tells us. "But if ye persevere patiently, and guard against evil, then that will be a determining factor in all affairs".

Now consider this, stop and think for a moment, does any of these behaviour patterns identifies with your present character, and if so have you just realized it for the first time? And if this is the case, are you pleased with yourself?

And if you are not, what are you going to do about your situation now that Allah has guided you to the meaning of one of his most blameworthy attributes that any human being could possess? Because this is clear proof that you have lost the ability to be patient in adversities which is the praiseworthy title of the believers, and the proof of this credit is in the statement of Allah.

َيَٰٓأَيُّهَا ٱلَّذِينَ ءَامَنُوا۟ ٱصْبِرُوا۟ وَصَابِرُوا۟ وَرَابِطُوا۟ وَٱتَّقُوا۟ ٱللَّهَ لَعَلَّكُمْ تُفْلِحُونَ

O ye who believe! Endure, outdo all others in endurance in Patience, be ready, and observe your duty to Allah, in order that ye may succeed. (HQ 3/200)

Patience, perseverance, constancy, self-restrain, refusing to bow down to the base desire of anger, which can lead to fitnah, are virtues to be exercised and practiced by the seekers of righteousness, especially in relation to others.

We set an example, so that they the people may vie (reason) with us, and we are to reason with them, lest we fall short of enjoining the good and forbidding the evil.

In this way we strengthen each other and bind our mutual relations closer, in our common service to Allah. We develop the ability to listen, and listen for benefit, and we learn to empathize rather than to talk and give useless advice. This is the model of our beloved Prophet (pbuh), who listens for the good of mankind, and by following this noble example we will become listeners for benefit.

Whenever Allah uses the word "Falah", translates prosperity or success, is to be understood in a wider context which includes both prosperity in our mundane affairs as well as in spiritual progress. In both cases it implies happiness and the attainment of our wishes while purifying our love for Allah Subhanahu wa ta-Allah, who has guided us to the seraatul-mustakeem, by following the examples of our beloved Prophet Mohammed (pbuh).

لَّقَدْ كَانَ لَكُمْ فِى رَسُولِ ٱللَّهِ أُسْوَةٌ حَسَنَةٌ لِّمَن كَانَ يَرْجُواْ ٱللَّهَ وَٱلْيَوْمَ ٱلْءَاخِرَ وَذَكَرَ ٱللَّهَ كَثِيرًا

Verily in the messenger of Allahye have a good example for him who looked unto Allah and the Last Day, and remembered Allah much. (33/21)

Ihtidaal: Praiseworthy anger is anger expressed in moderation. It is the anger which waits for the indication of the intellect and the deen. It arises when it is praised by the sharee'ah, and it stops when it is criticized by the sharee'ah. It is the middle way which the Messenger of Allah (pbuh) described when he said, "the best of affairs is their middle".

Any person who has insufficient anger must treat themselves until their anger becomes stronger to be used justly for the cause of Allah. Whoever lets their anger go to excess must treat themselves until it returns to the middle way between the two extremes, remembering the day of accountability, and Allah do not like extremist.

That is the Straight Path, (and this is what we as Muslims ask Allah for at least between 17 & 34 times per day, when we say "Ehdinas seratual Mustakeem". What are the two extremes referred to here by the Messenger of Allah? (pbuh) They are Tafreet Insufficient Anger, and Ifrat Excessive Anger)

This is the base from which the wisdom and the foundation of al-Walla and al-Barra'a are derived, which are two of the necessary attributes of eemaan.

An example of justifiable anger expressed or implied is when the people of Tawheed are witnessing the worshiping of any aspect of the creation being it human or other than them.

The Cure for Anger

To reflect on the virtues of restraining rancour, and to be patient during persecution, and to desire the reward for doing so. Allah says:

لَتُبْلَوُنَّ فِى أَمْوَالِكُمْ وَأَنفُسِكُمْ وَلَتَسْمَعُنَّ مِنَ ٱلَّذِينَ أُوتُوا۟ ٱلْكِتَٰبَ مِن قَبْلِكُمْ وَمِنَ ٱلَّذِينَ أَشْرَكُوٓا۟ أَذًى كَثِيرًا ۚ وَإِن تَصْبِرُوا۟ وَتَتَّقُوا۟ فَإِنَّ ذَٰلِكَ مِنْ عَزْمِ ٱلْأُمُورِ

You shall certainly be tried and tested in your wealth and properties and in your personal selves, and you shall certainly hear much that will grieve you from those who received the Scripture before you and from those who ascribe partners to Allah, but if you persevere patiently, and become Al-Muttaqûn (the pious) then verily, that will be a determining factor in all affairs, and that is from the great matters, [which you must hold on with all your efforts]. (3/186)

(2) Another virtue is to have the desire of maintaining peace between two or more people and desire the reward.

(3) To frighten oneself with the punishment of Allah, saying "The power of Allah over me is greater than my power over this person, and if I carry out my anger against him, then what security will I have against the anger of Allah on the Day of Qiyamah?"

(4) To reflect and make yourself fear the results of anger in this world if you have no fear of the next world. (This is for the person who has weak eemaan). This is the type of anger that may lead you to enmity between yourself and even loved ones, resulting in loss of life and property, prison and death row.

(5) To remember the ugliness of someone else's form when they are angry. Then you will realize how ugly you are during your state of anger. Reflect as well on how much you resemble the mad awliyaa of Iblis when you abandon self-restraint and control, and how much you resemble the awliyaa of Allah when you abandon your anger. For the peaceful believer and friend of Allah exercises patience.

(6) To reflect on or think about the cause which summons you to anger and revenge. It could be the whisper of Shaytaan, and this will only earn you immense incapacity and humiliation in the eyes of people. Therefore, you must reflect since you are more insignificant with Allah, the angels, and the Prophets. Why then are you concerned with people? So, the believer remembers to say at this point. I seek refuge in Allah from the accurst Shaytaan and then he recites the 114 chapter of the Holy Quran with lips and heart.

قُلْ أَعُوذُ بِرَبِّ ٱلنَّاسِ (١) مَلِكِ ٱلنَّاسِ (٢) إِلَٰهِ ٱلنَّاسِ (٣) مِن شَرِّ ٱلْوَسْوَاسِ ٱلْخَنَّاسِ ٤) ٱلَّذِى يُوَسْوِسُ فِى صُدُورِ ٱلنَّاسِ (٥) مِنَ ٱلْجِنَّةِ وَٱلنَّا

Say: I seek refuge in the Lord of mankind, (1) The King of mankind, (2) The God of mankind, (3) From the evil of the sneaking whisperer, (4) Who whispers in the hearts of mankind, (5) Of the jinn and of mankind. (HQ 114)

You should also reflect on the fact that your anger arises from your amazement at something which is acting in conformity with the will of Allah. It is almost as if Allah's anger with you is greater than your own anger. Remember everything happens by the will of Allah, even your own action, but it is not Allah who causes you to be angry. This is where the Kadariyah has gone astray; they think that it is Allah who causes mankind to commit sins. The Messenger of Allah (pbuh) says anger is from the heat of the Shaytaan.

As far as the action-cure is concerned, it is to say when you are angry, "I seek refuge with Allah from the accursed Shaytaan." If you are standing, then sit down. If you are sitting, then lie down, and do Wudu or Ghusl." When the Messenger of Allah (pbuh) was instructing this Ummah on what sets the soul free and what destroys it, he said "Whoever makes Wudu in the same way that I have just made Wudu, then stands up and pray two Raaka not thinking of other things, then his previous sins are forgiven."

He (pbuh) also says in a Hadith related by Abu Maalik Al-Ashaaree: "Purification is half of eemaan, and al-Hamdolillaa, fills the scale and Subhanah Allah and Al Hamdolillaa, fills whatever is between the Heavens and the Earth, and prayer is a light, Sadaqah is a clear proof, and sabr is a shining light, and the

Quran is a proof for or against you.

Every person starts his day dealing for his own Soul, so he either sets it free or he destroys it." Here the Messenger of Allah (pbuh) tells us of six of the most pleasing actions to Allah, and then he differentiates between the light of prayer and the light of patience, by saying prayer is a light, but patience is a shining light, this is the attribute that attracts the attention of the people around you.

Let us look at the varying degrees of desires that Allah has given to his created beings. According to our scholar Katadah, may Allah be pleased with him, "Allah created the angel with reason and no desire; he created the animal with desires and no reason; and he created man with both reason and desire. Therefore, if a man's reason is stronger than his desire, he behaves like an angel, but if his desire is stronger than his reason he behaves like an animal." The desire is propelled by pleasure and pain. Allah and his Prophet (pbuh) tell us repeatedly of the importance of patience and its ultimate reward with Allah. So, let us examine some of the virtues of patience.

If patience consists of restraining one's sexual desire, it is called honour, the opposite of which is adultery and promiscuity.

If it consists of restraining one's appetite, it is called self-control, the opposite of which is gluttony.

If it consists of keeping quiet about a thing which is not fit to be disclosed, it is called discretion, the opposite of which is slandering, backbiting, lying, and disclosing secrets.

If it consists of being content with what is sufficient of one's needs, it is called abstemiousness, the opposite of which is covetousness.

If it consists of controlling one's anger, it is called forbearance, the opposite of which is impulsiveness and hasty actions.

If it consists of refraining from haste, it is called gracefulness, and steadiness, the opposite of which is hot headiness.

If it consists of refraining from running away, it is called courage, the opposite of which is called cowardice.

If it consists of refraining from taking revenge, it is called forgiveness, the opposite of which is revenge.

If it consists of refraining from being stingy, it is called generosity, and the opposite of which is miserliness and negligence.

If it consists of refraining of being lazy and helplessness, it is called dynamism and initiative.

If it consists of refraining from blaming and accusing other people, it is called chivalry, liberty and manliness.

The Tongue

Be careful of the harvest of the tongue, for it expresses what is in the heart, and if a person's heart is good, you will see it in their saying.

Therefore, those who guard their tongue and use it for the purpose it was created for - enjoining good and forbidding evil, the dhikr of Allah, teaching the ignorant, worshipping Allah, reading the Quran, and giving sincere advice to the believers, to name a few.

This will get us closer to Allah, and will gain His good pleasure, but if we allow it to be engaged in vain and loose talk, we will sew the seed of our own destruction. It is true that one saying may enter a person into Jahannam, and one saying may save a person from the fire and enter one into Jannah.

From one of the many things which Allah has enjoined on His servants is the commanding of good and the forbidding of evil. As regards, the heart Allah has commanded us to love Him and His Messenger (pbuh), to love the good people, to love all that which Allah loves and to hate all that which Allah hates. It is the same regarding the tongue, there are things ordered and prohibited.

We have mentioned the commandment of Allah regarding the tongue. The prohibitions of the tongue are that you do not lie, abuse, use foul language, backbite, and do no slander. This tongue must be closed within this small prison that Allah has created. The tongue is protected by the teeth then the lips which should act as a prison when indulging in loose talk.

Another great example is the man who came to the Messenger of Allah (pbuh) and asked him to advise him, the Messenger of Allah (pbuh) replied "Do not get angry." The man again asked the Messenger of Allah (pbuh) "advise me," he (pbuh) replied "Do not get angry." The man asked again for the third time "Messenger of Allah (pbuh), advise me," the Messenger of Allah (pbuh) said again "Do not get angry."

There are overwhelming evidences that one of the primary causes of Fitnah within the family structure comes about as a result of anger. So once again I hope this small thesis that has been drawn from the Book of Allah and the Sunnah of the Messenger of Allah (pbuh) and extracts from the writings of the scholars of Islam may serve as a means of controlling the great enemy of mankind (Ghadab).

This summary identifies the people who restrain themselves, by protecting their tongue, their eyes, and ears, their hands and feet, their private parts, and their heart from evil, while enjoining the good, fearing Allah and the last day

Therefore, different names may be applied in different situations to the application of enjoining good, while remaining conscious of the opposite, for this is the playing field of Iblis, and we seek refuge in Allah from him and his host, but they are all linked to the practice of patience, so this shows that Islam in its totality is based on patience.

If a person does not possess these qualities, he should begin to realize his own deficiency and then start acting as if he possessed them, and eventually it will become second nature, this is the cure. (wa tawaasaw bill haqq, wa tawaasaw bi-sabr).

Conclusion

So, finally I ask Allah to whom there is no deity worthy to be worshipped in truth, to accept this humble offering of mine as an effort to bring me closer to Him, to gain His forgiveness and good pleasure in this life and the hereafter.

May it also be a benefit to those who read it while seeking the truth and those who experience the effect of those who have read it, as the Holy Prophet (pbuh) said "Patience is a shining light." And peace and blessings of Allah be upon our beloved Prophet Mohammed (pbuh), his family, his companions, and all those who follow him until the day of the rising.

Ameen.

Glossary

(A)

Abd ~ is servant, and is often used w when referring to a Muslim as the servant of Allah Abu ~ is father of.

Adabh ~ is used in reference to the behaviour and manners of an individual.

Aqedah ~ is creed.

Assabeya ~ is the term used to describe anyone who calls to nationalism, racism, etc. at the exclusion of other nationals, tribe, race, or cast.

Al walla'a wal Bara'a

(B)

Biddah ~ is innovation in the religion of Islam

(D)

Dayooth ~ is a man who permits the women under his care to exposes parts of their bodies that are Islamic Legislated to be covered in public, like hair, ears, legs, and arms, or he permits them to dress in a seductive way exposing the contour of her body without any objection.

Deen ~ is religion.

Dhikr ~ is the oral act of worship, for example like making statements which glorify Allah, or remembering Allah in the heart and calling on His names and Attributes.

Dhua'a ~ is to supplicate or ask Allah for whatever one requires.

Dunya ~ The material things of this world.

(E)

Eid ~ are two days in the Islamic calendar on which the Muslim nations of the world celebrate. First is the completion or breaking of the fast of Ramadan, and second is the tenth of the lunar month of Dhul-Hujjah, when the Muslims are performing Hajj.

Eemaan ~ is believing. According to the Prophet Muhammad (pbuh), eemaan is to believe in Allah, His angels, His books, His messengers, the Last Day, and qadar, the good and evil of it.

(F)

Faham ~ is comprehension or understanding.

Falah ~ is success.

Fatwa ~ is an Islamic ruling given by a scholar.

Fitnah ~ is test or temptation.

(G)

Ghadab ~ is anger.

Ghusl ~ is a ritual bath performed by Muslims on special occasions.

(H)

Hadith ~ is the reported saying and action of the Prophet Muhammad (pbuh)

Halal ~ approved as lawful, and fit for human consumption

Haram ~ is anything that Allah has forbidden.

Hawaah ~ is vain desires, fantasy, predilection, etc.

Hijab ~ is a scarf that covers the head, ears, neck, and chest of a woman.

(I)

Iblis ~ is one of the names of the dev.

Ihsaan ~ is the highest state of worship. According to the Prophet Muhammad (pbuh), "Ihsaan is to worship Allah as if you are seeing Him, knowing that you are not seeing Him, but He is seeing you." Imam ~ is one who leads.

Insha Allah ~ if Allah wills.

(J)

Jahannam ~ is one of the names of Hell.

Jaaliheyya ~ refers to the state or condition of a person or people while they are in a state of ignorance, i.e. Before being guided to Islam.

Jannah ~ Is one of the names of Paradise, Heaven, the Garden, etc.

Jilbab ~ is a covering for the parts of the human body that the Shariah (Islamic Law) legislate to be covered.

(K)

Khufu ~ is an adjective which is applicable to any person that believes and worships any aspect of the creation, rather than believing and worshipping Allah, the one true God, the Creator of all things, visible and invisible weather in the heavens or the Earth, the Forgiver, the moist Merciful.

(M)

Manhaj ~ is the methodology of the derivation, understanding, and application of the religion of Islam.

Masjid ~ is the house of Allah, where Muslims visit as an obligatory for the worship of the one true God, Allah.

Madhhab ~ is the name given to the different school of thoughts in Islam.

Madhabbies~ Followers of a specific school of thought,

(N)

Najas ~ Unclean and Islamic ally unlawful
Nushooz ~ To Elevate one's self over another
Naseeya ~ is advice.
Nikah~ is marriage.

(P)

PBUH ~ Peace be upon him. In Arabic, Salla Allah alyahi wa Sallam.

(Q)

Qiyamah ~ is one of the Quranic terms or names for the day of Judgement.

(R)

Rakah ~ A single unit of Salat.

Ramadan ~ is the ninth month of the Islamic calendar and it is the most meritorious month of the whole year because in this month the worship of Allah is maximised than any other month of the year. It is a month of fasting which is one of the pillars of Islam. In this month any Muslims who want to achieve the great reward that Allah have promised to the believers must restrain themselves from all forms of evil action. All acts of worship are maximized such as the prayers, especially at night, giving charity, restraining one's anger, and do all acts of worship that will bring the believer closer to Allah.

(S)

Salaf~ linguistically means predecessors, and in Islamic context refers to the first, second, and third generation of Muslims, the Sahabah, Companions of the prophet Mohammed (pbuh), the tabi'een, and the tabi'een At-tabi'een, respectively. The second generation after the Prophet and his companions.

Shaykh ~ is a learned Islamic scholar, or a man who has reached the age of fifty.

Salat ~ Prayer

Shaytaan ~ is one of the names of the devil.

Shariah ~ is the Arabic name for Islamic Law.

Shia ~ One of the seventy-two sects in Islam, the most dominant of which is found in Iran.

Sunnah ~ is the sayings and actions of the Prophet Mohammed (pbuh) and things and things which he saw and heard and approved.

(T)

Talaq ~ To Divorce, or legally setting a woman free from the ties of marriage

(U)

Ullamah ~ are the scholars of Islam (successors of the Prophet pbuh) in terms of knowledge) and it is they who rectify the affairs of the Muslims.

Ummah ~ All the people that have and will respond to the call of Islam that Prophet Mohammed (pbuh). The seal of the prophets) brought to men and Jinns to the end of time.

(W)

Wakeel ~ is the representative of a woman while she is contracting a marriage, in the absence of her father, uncle, brother, or son.

Walli ~ is the father, uncle, brother, or son of a woman who act as her guardian. He is one of the pillars on which the legality of a marriage is based.

Wajib ~ That which is made obligatory upon a Muslim.

www.ingramcontent.com/pod-product-compliance
Lightning Source LLC
Chambersburg PA
CBHW061732070526
44583CB00024B/3115